Isle of Man Shipping
The Twilight Years

Isle of Man Shipping
The Twilight Years

Ian Collard

Lady of Mann (1930/3,104grt) at sea.

First published 2001
Reprinted 2004, 2011, 2019

The History Press
The Mill, Brimscombe Port
Stroud, Gloucestershire GL5 2QG
www.thehistorypress.co.uk

© Ian Collard, 2001

The right of Ian Collard to be identified as the Author
of this work has been asserted in accordance with the
Copyrights, Designs and Patents Act 1988.

All rights reserved. No part of this book may be reprinted
or reproduced or utilised in any form or by any electronic,
mechanical or other means, now known or hereafter invented,
including photocopying and recording, or in any information
storage or retrieval system, without the permission in writing
from the Publishers.

British Library Cataloguing in Publication Data.
A catalogue record for this book is available from the British Library.

ISBN 978 0 7524 2131 5

Typesetting and origination by Tempus Publishing.
Printed and bound by TJ International Limited, Padstow, Cornwall

Contents

Acknowledgements		6
Introduction		7
1.	Douglas	9
2.	Ramsey, Ardrossan, Belfast, Dublin and Heysham	55
3.	Llandudno	61
4.	Mersey Docks	73
5.	Cargo Vessels	113
6.	Fastcats	125

Acknowledgements

I wish to thank Capt. Peter Corrin, Marine Operations Manager of the Isle of Man Steam Packet Company, and Tony Kennish of the Ramsey Steamship Company for all their help in the preparation of this book. I would also like to acknowledge the kind assistance given by Adrian Sweeney, John Luxton, the Manxman Steamship Company and Ships of Mann.

King Orry(1946/ 2,485grt) arrives at Douglas from Ardrossan.

Introduction

The Isle of Man Steam Packet has been operating shipping services from the Isle of Man since 1830. Their first steamer *Mona's Isle* (1) was built on the River Clyde for the Douglas to Liverpool service and sailed her maiden voyage on 16 August 1830. It was originally called The Mona's Isle Co. but the name was changed to the Isle of Man Steam Packet Co. in 1832.

Steam Packet vessels saw service in both World Wars. *King Orry* (3) became an armed boarding vessel and later a target towing ship during the First World War. In 1914 *Peel Castle* (1) was converted to an armed boarding vessel and employed in convoy duties throughout the war.

Of the fifteen vessels owned by the Steam Packet in 1914 eleven were taken over by the Admiralty. Only seven of these were in service at the end of the war in 1919 and the Company chartered the Liverpool & North Wales Steamship Co.'s paddle steamer *La Marguerite* to maintain services to the Island.

On 5 April 1927 *Ben My Chree* (4) was launched by Cammell Laird & Co. Ltd at Birkenhead. Over her years of service with the Company she proved a very successful steamer and an asset to the fleet. In 1932 her appearance was changed when her hull was painted white for a charter. During the Second World War *Ben My Chree* was engaged on troop transport duties in the English Channel and the Faroe Islands. In 1944 she was at Omaha Beach as the Headquarters for the 514 Assault Flotilla.

In 1930 the Steam Packet celebrated its centenary and introduced their largest vessel into the fleet. *Lady of Mann* (1) was built by Vickers Armstrong Ltd at Barrow-in-Furness and was launched by the Lady of Mann, Her Grace the Duchess of Athol, on 4 March that year. In 1933 her hull was also painted white and during the Second World War she sailed together with her sister *Ben My Chree* in the English Channel and to the Faroe Islands.

Mona's Queen (3) was launched by Cammell Laird at Birkenhead on 12 April 1934. She was similar to *Lady of Mann* and *Ben My Chree* except that she had her promenade deck extended forward to the bow. After a very short career with the Steam Packet she went to war, only to hit a mine and sink at Dunkirk on 29 May 1940.

In 1936 Vickers Armstrong at Barrow launched two sister ships for the Company, *Fenella* (2) and *Tynwald* (4). Their design formed the basis for the class of five sisters built immediately after the Second World War. Both vessels were taken over by the Admiralty in 1939. *Fenella* was bombed during an air attack at Dunkirk on 29 May 1940 and sank. *Tynwald* became an anti-aircraft ship and was fitted with high angle guns. In November 1942 she was torpedoed and sank at Bougie, Algeria.

Passenger services to the Isle of Man were maintained by the *Rushen Castle* (1), *Victoria* (1) and later *Snaefell* (4) from Fleetwood during the Second World War. In 1945 the Steam Packet fleet consisted of nine passenger vessels *Viking* (1), *Manxman* (1), *Snaefell*, *Mona's Isle*, *Manx Maid* (1), *Ben My Chree* (4), *Victoria* (1), *Lady of Mann* (1) and *Rushen Castle* (1). The Company also operated two cargo vessels *Peveril* (2) and *Conister* (1).

On 8 April 1946 services to the Island were transferred back to Liverpool from Fleetwood and on 18 April the new *King Orry* (4) sailed on her maiden voyage from Liverpool to Douglas. She was the first of a class of five passenger steamers to enter service which were all built by Cammell Laird at Birkenhead.

Mona's Queen was launched on 5 February 1946, *Tynwald* on 24 March 1947, *Snaefell* on 11 March 1948 and *Mona's Isle* on 12 October 1950. *Manxman*, the last steamer of the class, sailed on her maiden voyage on 21 May 1955.

The Isle of Man Steam Packet's first car ferry *Manx Maid* (2) was launched on 23 January 1962. She was designed as a side-loader and incorporated a series of special ramps which allowed vehicles to be loaded and unloaded at any state of the tide at Douglas. She was followed into service in 1966 by an almost identical sister ship, *Ben My Chree* (5). In 1972 the diesel powered *Mona's Queen* (5) was introduced and her sister *Lady of Mann* (2) was launched by the Ailsa Shipbuilding Co. at Troon on 4 December 1975.

In 1978 Geoff Duke and a group of other Manx businessmen formed Manx Line to provide modern roll on/roll off services to the island. They chartered the Spanish car-ferry *Monte Castillo*, which was renamed *Manx Viking*, and inaugurated a new service from Heysham to Douglas on 26 August 1978. Later that year the company was taken over by Sealink and James Fisher.

The Steam Packet and Manx Line continued to provide seperate services to the island until 1985, when a merger of operations was announced with sailings provided from Heysham and the closure of the Liverpool to Douglas route.

The service was provided by *Manx Viking* and *Mona's Isle* (6), which was withdrawn in October 1985 and replaced by *Antrim Princess*, which was renamed *Tynwald* (6). *Manx Viking* was withdrawn in September 1986 and sold to Norwegian owners the following year. *Mona's Isle* was renamed *Al Fahad* when she was sold to Saudi Arabian owners and sailed from Birkenhead to the Red Sea on 7 April 1986.

Tynwald (6) remained in service until 1990 when the *Channel Entente* was purchased by the Steam Packet and renamed *King Orry* (5). *Lady of Man* (2) was replaced by the 74m catamaran *Seacat Isle of Man* that was chartered from Seacontainers and sailed on her maiden voyage from Douglas to Fleetwood on 28 June 1994.

Seacontainers took a controlling interest in the Steam Packet in 1996 and two years later intorduced the ro-pax vessel *Ben My Chree* (6) and various fast craft, car and passenger vessels to their Irish Sea operations. They have also provided new services from England and Scotland to Northern Ireland and the Republic of Ireland with their fast Seacat ferries, offering the highest standards of comfort and service. *Lady of Mann* returned to service providng winter relief sailings and various special and charter sailings in the Irish Sea and the Azores.

One

Douglas

Douglas is the capital of the Isle of Man. It is the main seaport and gateway to the Island for passengers arriving by sea. In the 1960s, the main shipping operator was the Isle of Man Steam Packet Co. who operated services to Liverpool, Heysham, Fleetwood, Llandudno, Ardrossan, Dublin and Belfast.

In this period Douglas was one of Britain's leading holiday resorts providing a variety of leisure, sporting and recreational facilities along its two miles of sandy beach. The Palace, the Villa Marina with magnificent ballrooms and music by leading dance bands, cinemas, concert halls and theatres all provided a variety of entertainments for the visitor.

In June and September each year motorcyclists arrived in their thousands from all over the world for the Tourist Trophy and Senior races. Golf, cycling and sailing facilities were all provided for the tourist on the Island.

Visitors arriving by sea embark at the Victoria or Edward Piers in the harbour after their ferry had passed the breakwater and usually swung around to berth at the link span. In the 1960s Douglas Harbour tended to be a hive of activity, with the early morning steamers taking passengers, cars, and day excursion visitors to Liverpool, Dublin or Belfast. At lunch-time the steamer from Liverpool would berth and other visitors would arrive from Llandudno and Fleetwood for a day on the Island.

On Saturdays in the summer season most of the steamers were needed to take holidaymakers home and bring new visitors to the Island. There would be two or three sailings to Liverpool in the morning and the first arrival from the mainland would normally take the afternoon sailing to Ardrossan in Scotland. Sunday was a day of rest for the steamers and most of the ships' crews would enjoy a day berthed in the harbour at Douglas.

Low water at Douglas Harbour with *Manxman* (1955/2,495grt) resting at the South Edward Pier on a summer Sunday in 1968.

Tynwald (1947/2,493grt), *Manx Maid* (1962/2,724grt) and *Mona's Isle* (1951/2,491grt) at the Victoria Pier. *Lady of Mann* (1930/3,104grt) and *Manxman* (1955/2,495grt) are berthed at the Edward Pier.

Stella Marina (1965/1,588grt) arrives at Douglas from Fleetwood in June 1969.

Lady of Mann (1930/3,104grt), *Tynwald* (1947/2,493grt) and *Manx Maid* (1962/2,724grt) at Victoria Pier. *King Orry* (1946/2,485grt) and *Mona's Isle* (1951/2,491grt) at the Edward Pier with the cargo vessel *Ramsey* (1965/446grt).

Treat yourself to a day long Luxury Mini Cruise from Fleetwood to the

ISLE OF MAN

on the air-conditioned Mini Liner STELLA MARINA

FOR TIMES OF SAILING SEE OVER!

Or take a Starlight Cruise in Morecambe Bay 25/-

Depart Fleetwood approx 22.30 hours
Return approx 02.00 hours

SEE OVER FOR COMPLETE BOOKING FORM!

Details of the Norwest Hovercraft Fleetwood to Douglas service operated by *Stella Marina* in 1969 and *Norwest Laird* in 1970.

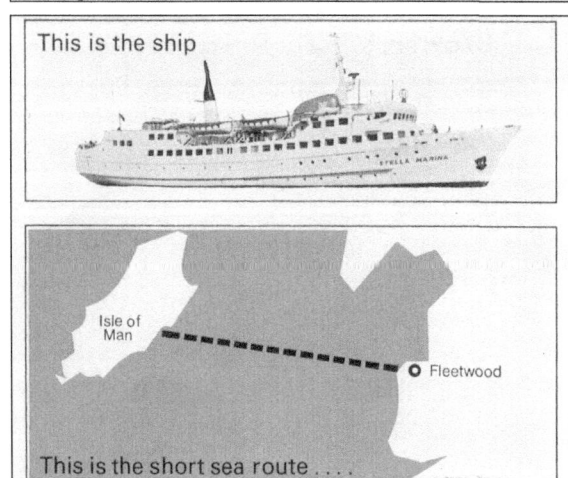

This is the ship

Isle of Man — Fleetwood

This is the short sea route....

1970 Timetable and Fares

Timetable
Fleetwood – Isle of Man

	Every day May 8 – September 20	Additional Sailings when necessary
Depart Fleetwood	10.30	12 midnight
Arrive Isle of Man	14.00	04.30
Depart Isle of Man	18.00	05.30
Arrive Fleetwood	21.30	09.00

Fares

	Adult	Child	
Day return	50/-	25/-	
Mid week return	70/-	35/-	Valid until end of 1970
Weekend return	80/-	40/-	Valid until end of 1970
Single	47/6	24/-	

Single journey rates

		£	s	d
Vehicles *overall length as in manufacturers lists* under ft. ins.				
10 6			4	10	0
11 6			5	10	0

and thereafter 20/- for each additional foot

Norwest Laird (1939/577grt) arrives at the Edward Pier from Fleetwood in 1970. She was sold in 1974 and laid up at Hayle in Cornwall. In 1978 she was renamed *Lochiel* and moved to Bristol, where she remained until 1996 when she was broken up.

Fenella (1951/1,019grt) and *Peveril* (1964/1,048grt) unload general cargo at the Steam Packet berth in Douglas Harbour.

A seagull follows *Snaefell* (1948/2,489grt) as she sets course for North Wales on a return day sailing to Llandudno in 1966.

Ben My Chree (1927/2,586grt) arrives from Liverpool in August 1960.

THE ISLE OF MAN STEAM PACKET COMPANY LIMITED
(INCORPORATED IN THE ISLE OF MAN)

Telegrams: STEAMERS, DOUGLAS   Telephone · DOUGLAS 1101

PASSENGER SERVICES
JANUARY 1st to APRIL 30th, 1963
(INCLUDING EASTER)

The Company may alter, withdraw, or curtail any service or suspend or cancel any sailing as the Company may think necessary.

LIVERPOOL AND DOUGLAS
(4 Hours)

LIVERPOOL to DOUGLAS	DOUGLAS to LIVERPOOL
Weekdays to April 10th .... 11 a.m.	Weekdays to April 10th .... 9 a.m.
Thursday, April 11th .... 11 a.m. & 3-30 p.m.	Thursday, April 11th .... 9 a.m., 4 p.m. & 12 night
Friday, April 12th .... 1 a.m. & 11 a.m.	Friday, April 12th ...... 9 a.m. & 12 night
Saturday, April 13th ...... 1 a.m. & 11 a.m.	Saturday, April 13th .... 9 a.m.
Sunday, April 14th .... 1 a.m.	Monday, April 15th ...... 9 a.m., 4 p.m. & 12 night
Monday, April 15th...11 a.m. & 3-30 p.m.	
Weekdays from April 16th ....11 a.m.	Weekdays from April 16th .... 9 a.m.

★ DAY EXCURSIONS ★
During Easter Holidays

From LIVERPOOL	Returning from DOUGLAS
Thursday, April 11th .... 11 a.m.	4 p.m. or 12 night
Friday, April 12th .... 1 a.m. or 11 a.m.	12 night
Monday, April 15th .... 11 a.m.	4 p.m. or 12 night

From DOUGLAS	Returning from LIVERPOOL
Thursday, April 11th .... 9 a.m.	3-30 p.m. Thursday or 1 a.m. Friday
Thursday, April 11th .... 12 night	1 a.m. Saturday
Friday, April 12th .... 9 a.m.	
Friday, April 12th .... 12 night	1 a.m. Sunday
Saturday, April 13th .... 9 a.m.	
Monday, April 15th .... 9 a.m.	3-30 p.m. Monday

---

Passenger Fares:

SINGLE	FIRST CLASS 38/-	SECOND CLASS 30/-
RETURN (3 Months)	FIRST CLASS 65/-	SECOND CLASS 55/-
DAY EXCURSION	FIRST CLASS 26/-	SECOND CLASS 22/-

MID-WEEK ... FIRST CLASS 55/-; SECOND CLASS 45/-
These tickets will be available for travel outwards on Tuesday, Wednesday or Thursday and return on either Tuesday, Wednesday or Thursday within a period of three months.

CHILDREN under 3 years of age, FREE; 3 years and under 14, HALF-FARE
Infants must be accompanied by an adult.

SPECIAL WINTER CONTRACT TICKET—First Class, Three Months, £8.5.0.

Combined steamer and rail tickets to principal railway stations in Great Britain can be purchased at the Company's Offices.

Meals and Refreshments available.

Passengers and their accompanied luggage will only be carried subject to the Company's Standard Conditions of Carriage of Passengers and Passengers Accompanied Property as exhibited in the Company's Offices and on board its vessels.

Acceptance of a ticket issued by the Company binds the passenger to these conditions.

AGENTS: THOS. ORFORD & SON, INDIA BUILDINGS,
40, BRUNSWICK STREET, LIVERPOOL, 2. Tel.: Central 3214.

Imperial Buildings,   A. J. FICK,
Douglas, October, 1962.   General Manager.

Details of the January to April sailings on the Liverpool to Douglas route in 1963.

Lady of Mann (1930/3,104grt) turns off Douglas Head on a voyage to Liverpool.

Manxman (1955/2,495grt) moves full astern at the start of a voyage to Ardrossan, Scotland, as *Mona's Isle* (1951/2,491grt) arrives from Dublin.

Steam Packet vessels rest in Douglas Harbour on a warm summer's day in 1968 after bringing vehicles, tourists and day trippers to the Island.

Lady of Mann (1930/3,104grt) prepares to take the return 1600 sailing to Liverpool.

The Liverpool & North Wales Steamship Co. *St Seriol* (1931/1,586grt) operated sailings from Llandudno, North Wales, to Douglas. In 1961 the company went into voluntary liquidation and *St Seriol* was sold for scrap. (Liverpool & North Wales Steamship Co.)

On Sundays during the summer season most of the Steam Packet fleet enjoyed a day off berthed in Douglas Harbour. Here seven passenger vessels occupy berths at the Victoria and Edward Piers while *Fenella* loads cargo at the freight berth.

'For Sale' notice for *Mona's Queen* (1945/2,485grt) and reported sale to the Chandris Group in 1962, for service as a cruise ship in the Adriatic.

> Another interesting sale during the week, reported in the general news columns of *The Journal of Commerce and Shipping Telegraph* last Tuesday, concerns the Isle of Man Steam Packet Co. turbine passenger vessel Mona's Queen (2,485 gross tons). She has been bought by a Liberian associate of the Chandris group, Marivic Navigation Inc. and has given prompt delivery Barrow and been renamed Barrow Queen.

> Mona's Queen, passenger steamer, 2,485 g.r.t., 953 n.r.t. Built Birkenhead 1946. Sold by Isle of Man Steam Packet Co., Douglas, to Marivic Navigation Inc., a Liberian affiliate of the Chandris group. She will give prompt delivery at Barrow and is being renamed Barrow Queen.

S.S. MONAS QUEEN.

REPORTED SALE OF THE MONAS QUEEN TO A GREEK SHIPPING COMPANY FOR CRUISING IN THE ADRIATIC.

FOR SALE
UNDER INSTRUCTIONS FROM THE
ISLE OF MAN STEAM PACKET CO.
LTD.
The Twin Screw Turbine
Passenger Steamer

"MONA'S QUEEN"

About 2,485 tons gross. Built 1946. Classed Lloyd's A.1 Irish Channel service S.S. 3/59.
4 Steam Turbines. Speed 26 knots. 1,019 First and 1,144 Second Class passengers.
DIMS.: Abt. 345' O.A.; 335' 10" B.P. x 47' 2" x 17' 2" — 18' Mld.
(Not accountable for errors in description)
Inspectable Barrow-in-Furness.
Further particulars on application to:—
C. W. KELLOCK & CO. LTD.,
27-31, St. Mary Axe,   Cunard Building,
LONDON, E.C.3.   LIVERPOOL, 3.
Telegrams: "KELLOCKS"

HMS *Duncan*, HMS *Keppel* and the passenger liner *Völkerfreundschaft* anchored in Douglas Bay on 15 June 1968. *Völkerfreundschaft* was built as the *Stockholm*, owned by the Swedish-America Line. On 25 July 1956 she collided with the new Italian liner *Andrea Doria* in thick fog 100 miles off New York. The *Andrea Doria* sank with the loss of 47 lives. Five people also died on the *Stockholm*, which was able to reach New York under her own power. In 1960 she was bought by the Free German Trades Union Confederation and renamed *Völkerfreundschaft*, and was used for cruising.

Mona's Isle (1951/2,491grt) moves astern in the harbour while *Manxman* (1955/2,495grt) loads passengers for a sailing to Belfast in 1965.

Lady of Mann (1930/3,104grt) remained in service with the Steam Packet until 1971 when she was broken up in Dalmuir.

Ben My Chree (1966/2,762grt), *Mona's Isle* (1951/2,491grt), *Tynwald* (1947/2,493grt) and *Manxman* (1955/2,495grt) have a day off in June, 1968.

ALL TRAFFIC CARRIED SUBJECT TO THE STANDARD CONDITIONS OF CARRIAGE OF THE COMPANY AS EXHIBITED IN ITS OFFICES AND ON BOARD ITS VESSELS.

The Isle of Man Steam Packet Co. Limited

(INCORPORATED IN THE ISLE OF MAN)

P.O. BOX No. 5

TELEGRAMS:
"STEAMERS, DOUGLAS."

TELEPHONE No.
DOUGLAS 3824

TELEX 62414
STEAMERS, DOUGLAS

Imperial Buildings,
Douglas, Isle of Man.

OUR REFERENCE   YOUR REFERENCE
A/.

31st July, 1971.

Dear Sir,

FLEETWOOD TO DOUGLAS SERVICE - 1971

The Engineering Contractors advise that the work on extending the berth at Fleetwood is progressing to time and should be completed sufficiently to permit steamer services to resume on 25th August.

Subject to berth availability, this Company is pleased to announce the following schedule of services for 1971.

		Depart Fleetwood	Depart Douglas
Wednesday,	25th August	1030 hrs.	1700 hrs.
Thursday,	26th "	"	"
Friday,	27th "	"	"
Sunday,	29th "	"	"
Monday,	30th "	"	"
Tuesday,	31st "	"	"
Wednesday,	1st September	"	"
Thursday,	2nd "	"	"
Sunday,	12th "	"	"
Monday,	13th "	"	"
Tuesday,	14th "	"	"

Time allowed ashore in the Isle of Man about 3½ hours.

It will be noted there are no sailings between Thursday, 2nd and Sunday, 12th September. This is due to operational difficulties which would seriously reduce the time ashore, hence we regret there will be no services.

The day excursion fare will be £2.50 return. Passengers travelling to the Isle of Man on holiday can use the services. The return fare is £5.20 unless both the inward and outward journeys are made on Tuesday, Wednesday or Thursday, in which event the fare is £4.70. Return portions of Fleetwood tickets are valid for return to Liverpool without extra charge and vice versa.

No motor vehicles can be conveyed. Any enquiries regarding the services should be addressed to the Head Office of the Company. For 1971 passenger tickets will only be available from British Transport Docks Board at Fleetwood. Agents' exchange vouchers will be accepted by the Booking Clerk. Reservations for Private Cabins should be made to the Head Office, at Douglas. For 1972 the Company intends to open the service about end of May and continue to mid-September. The frequency will be decided and published by the year-end, but will be mid-week with additional sailings on Sundays during the high season.

Yours faithfully,
S.R. SHIMMIN
General Manager

Letter from the Steam Packet detailing the resumption of the Fleetwood to Douglas service in 1971.

Passengers and cars are loaded onto the *Manxman* (1955/2,495grt) and *Lady of Mann* (1930/3,104grt) at the Edward Pier.

Tynwald (1947/2,487grt) and *King Orry* (1946/2,485grt) berthed together at Victoria Pier.

THE ISLE OF MAN STEAM PACKET COMPANY LIMITED

(Incorporated in the Isle of Man)

WELCOME RETURN OF THE
FLEETWOOD
TO DOUGLAS
STEAMER SERVICE

Enjoy a . . .

DAY EXCURSION

on

WEDNESDAY . 25th AUGUST	MONDAY . . . . . . 30th AUGUST
THURSDAY . . 26th AUGUST	TUESDAY . . . . . . 31st AUGUST
FRIDAY . . . . . 27th AUGUST	WEDNESDAY . 1st SEPTEMBER
SUNDAY . . . . 29th AUGUST	THURSDAY . . 2nd SEPTEMBER

also

SUNDAY 12th, MONDAY 13th and TUESDAY 14th SEPTEMBER

FLEETWOOD	**DOUGLAS**
Depart 10-30 a.m.	Depart 5-0 p.m.

Allowing about 3½ hours ashore in Douglas

DAY RETURN FARE £2.50

Children 3 and under 14 years Half-fare

Tickets obtainable from Booking Office alongside Steamer on day of Sailing

Passengers travelling to the Isle of Man on holiday can use the services. The return fare is £5.20 unless both the inward and outward journeys are made on Tuesday, Wednesday or Thursday, in which event the fare is £4.70. Return portions of Fleetwood tickets are valid for return to Liverpool without extra charge and vice versa. No motor vehicles can be conveyed. Any enquiries regarding the services should be addressed to the Head Office of the Company.

For 1972 the Company intends to open the service about end of MAY and continue to mid-September. The frequency will be decided and published by the year-end, but will be mid-week with additional sailings on Sundays during the high season.

All steamers are fully licensed and there are buffets for light refreshments.

The Company may alter, withdraw or curtail any service or suspend or cancel any sailing as the Company may think necessary.

PASSENGERS AND THEIR ACCOMPANIED LUGGAGE will only be carried subject to the Company's Standard Conditions of Carriage of Passengers and Passengers' Accompanied Property as exhibited in the Company's Offices and on board its vessels. Acceptance of a ticket issued by the Company binds the Passenger to these conditions.

IMPERIAL BUILDINGS, DOUGLAS.
Telephone 0624 3824

S. R. SHIMMIN, General Manager.
AUGUST, 1971.

B. & Hx. Ltd., I.O.M.

Brochure advertising the 'welcome' return of the Fleetwood to Douglas service in 1971.

Crew members 'touch-up' the paintwork on *Ben My Chree* (1966/2,762grt) as she enjoys a day off berthed at the Victoria Pier.

Ramsey (1965/446grt) was operated by the Steam Packet until 1974 when she was sold and renamed *Hoofort*. She became *Boa Entrado* in 1982 and *Arquipelago* in 1990.

Each passenger vessel in the Steam Packet fleet had their own personalized beer mats in the ship's bar.

Lady of Mann (1930/3,104grt) passes two naval vessels and a cargo ship berthed at the Battery Pier.

A view of the harbour from the Douglas Head café which has now been closed and demolished.

Liverpool and Douglas

1st MAY to 24th MAY

Liverpool to Douglas (3¾ hours) Douglas to Liverpool
Mondays to Saturdays   Mondays to Saturdays
    11 a.m.   9 a.m.

25th MAY to 31st MAY

Mondays to Saturdays   Mondays to Saturdays
  10.30 a.m. & 3.30 p.m.   9 a.m. and 4 p.m.
Sunday, 27th ...... 1 a.m.   Sunday, 27th ... 12 night

JUNE

Mondays to Fridays   Mondays to Thursdays
  10.30 a.m. & 3.30 p.m.   9 a.m. and 4 p.m.
Monday, 4th ...... 1 a.m.,   Monday, 4th ......
  10.30 a.m. & 3.30 p.m.   4 p.m. and 6 p.m.
Monday, 11th ...... 9 a.m.,   Wednesday, 6th ......
  10.30 a.m. & 3.30 p.m.   4 p.m and 6 p.m.
Wednesday, 6th ... 1 a.m.,   Wednesday, 27th ... 9 a.m.,
  10.30 a.m. & 3.30 p.m.   4 p.m. and 5.30 p.m.
Thursday, 28th ... 9 a.m.,   Fridays ... 9 a.m., 4 p.m.,
  10.30 a.m. & 3.30 p.m.   and 12 night
Friday, 8th ...... 1 a.m.,   Friday, 8th, 9 a.m., 4 p.m.,
  10.30 a.m. & 3.30 p.m.   6 p.m. & 12 night
Saturdays to 23rd, 1 a.m.,   Saturdays, 2nd, 16th & 23rd
  10 a.m., 11 a.m. and   9 a.m. and 4 p.m.
  3.30 p.m.   Saturday, 9th, 6.30 a.m.
Saturday, 30th ... 1 a.m., .   8 a.m., 9 a.m.,
  10 a.m., 11 a.m.,   4 p.m., 6 p.m. and
  1 p.m. and 3.30 p.m.   12 night.
Sundays ... 1 a.m. & 4 p.m.   Saturday, 30th ... 8 a.m.,
                                   9 a.m. and 4 p.m.
                              Sundays .... 9.30 a.m.

JULY

Mondays to Fridays   Mondays to Thursdays
  10.30 a.m. & 3.30 p.m.   9 a.m. and 4 p.m.
Thursdays .... 9 a.m.,   Weds., except 18th, 9 a.m.,
  10.30 a.m. & 3.30 p.m.   4 p.m. and 5.30 p.m.
Saturday, 7th ... 1 a.m.,   Fridays ... 9 a.m., 4 p.m.,
  10 a.m., 11 a.m.,   and 12 night
  1 p.m. and 3.30 p.m.   Saturday, 7th ... 8 a.m.,
Saturdays from 14th   9 a.m. and 4 p.m.
  1 a.m., 8 a.m., 9 a.m.,   Saturday, 14th 7.30 a.m.
  11 a.m., 1 p.m. and   8 a.m., 9 a.m. and
  3.30 p.m.   4 p.m.
Sundays ... 1 a.m. & 4 p.m.   Saturdays 21st and 28th
                                 6 a.m., 7 a.m.,
                                 8 a.m., 9 a.m. and
                                 4 p.m.
                              Sundays .... 9.30 a.m.

AUGUST

Mondays to Fridays   Mondays to Thursdays
  10.30 a.m. & 3.30 p.m.   9 a.m. and 4 p.m.
Monday, 6th ...... 1 a.m.,   Monday, 6th ...... 9 a.m.,
  10.30 a.m. & 3.30 p.m.   4 p.m. and 6 p.m.
Thursdays .... 9 a.m.,   Wednesdays ...... 9 a.m.,
  10.30 a.m. & 3.30 p.m.   4 p.m. and 5.30 p.m.
Saturdays, 4th & 11th   Fridays ... 9 a.m., 4 p.m.,
  1 a.m., 8 a.m., 9 a.m.,   and 12 night
  11 a.m., 1 p.m. and   Saturdays, 4th and 11th
  3.30 p.m.   6 a.m., 7 a.m.,
Saturdays 18th & 25th   8 a.m., 9 a.m. and
  1 a.m., 10 a.m., 11 a.m.,   4 p.m.
  1 p.m. and 3.30 p.m.   Saturdays, 18th & 25th
Sundays ... 1 a.m. & 4 p.m.   6.30 a.m., 7.30 a.m.,
                                   9 a.m. and 4 p.m.
                              Sundays .... 9.30 a.m.

Liverpool and Douglas

1st SEPTEMBER to 10th SEPTEMBER

Liverpool to Douglas   Douglas to Liverpool
Mondays to Fridays   Mondays to Thursdays
  10.30 a.m. & 3.30 p.m.   9 a.m. and 4 p.m.
Thursday, 6th ... 1 a.m.,   Friday, 7th ...... 9 a.m.,
  10.30 a.m. & 3.30 p.m.   4 p.m. and 12 night
Saturday, 1st   Saturdays, 1st and 8th
  1 a.m., 10 a.m.,   8 a.m., 9 a.m. and
  11 a.m. and 3.30 p.m.   4 p.m.
Saturday, 8th ...... 1 a.m., Sundays, 2nd & 9th
  10.30 a.m. & 3.30 p.m.   9.30 a.m.
Sundays, 2nd & 9th
  1 a.m. and 4 p.m.

11th SEPTEMBER to 30th SEPTEMBER

Weekdays .... 11 a.m.   Weekdays .... 9 a.m.
Sundays .... 1 a.m.   Friday, 14th
                                   9 a.m. and 12 night
                                Sunday, 16th ... 9.30 a.m.
                                Sundays, 23rd & 30th
                                                12 night

Dublin and Douglas

31st MAY to 11th SEPTEMBER

Dublin to Douglas (4¼ hours) Douglas to Dublin
Thursday, 31st May, 5 p.m.   Thurs., 31st May, 8.30 a.m.

JUNE

Wednesdays from 13th   Wednesdays from 13th
                     5 p.m.   8.30 a.m.
Thursday, 7th ...... 5 p.m.   Thursday, 7th ... 8.30 a.m.
Fridays from 15th ... 5 p.m.   Fridays from 15th 8.30 a.m.

JULY

Tuesday, 10th ...... 5 p.m.   Tuesday, 10th ... 8.30 a.m.
Wednesdays except 11th   Wednesdays, except 11th
                     5 p.m.   8.30 a.m.
Thursday, 12th ...... 5 p.m.   Thursday, 12th ... 8.30 a.m.
Fridays, except 13th, 5 p.m.   Fridays, except 13th
                                                8.30 a.m.

AUGUST

Monday, 6th .... 8 a.m.   Monday, 6th ... 7.30 p.m.
Wednesdays .... 5 p.m.   and 12 night.
Fridays .... 5 p.m. Wednesdays ...... 8.30 a.m.
Saturday, 4th ...... 12 night   Fridays .... 8.30 a.m.
                                Saturday, 4th ... 5.30 p.m.

SEPTEMBER

Wednesday, 5th ... 5 p.m.   Wednesday, 5th, 8.30 a.m.
Tuesday, 11th ...... 5 p.m.   Tuesday, 11th ... 8.30 a.m.

Steam Packet sailing brochure covering passenger sailings for the 1962 summer season.

Royal naval vessel P3104 arrives at Douglas on a weekend naval exercise.

King Orry (1946/2,485grt) and *Mona's Isle* (1951/2,491grt) at the Edward Pier.

ALL TRAFFIC CARRIED SUBJECT TO THE STANDARD CONDITIONS OF CARRIAGE OF THE COMPANY AS EXHIBITED IN ITS OFFICES AND ON BOARD ITS VESSELS

The Isle of Man Steam Packet Co. Limited.

(INCORPORATED IN THE ISLE OF MAN.)

P.O. BOX No. 5

TELEGRAMS: "STEAMERS, DOUGLAS."
TELEPHONE No. DOUGLAS 1101 (6 LINES)
TELEX 62414 STEAMERS, DOUGLAS

Imperial Buildings,
Douglas, Isle of Man.

OUR REFERENCE   YOUR REFERENCE

PRESENT FLEET

Steamer	Built	Gross Tonnage	Length Feet	Breadth Feet	Speed Knots
Lady of Mann	1930	3104	371	50	22½
Manx Maid	1962	2725	343	50	21
Ben-my-Chree	1927	2586	366	46	22
Manxman	1955	2495	344	47	21
Mona's Isle	1951	2491	344	47	21
Snaefell	1948	2489	344	47	21
Tynwald	1947	2493	344	47	21
King Orry	1946	2485	344	47	21
Peveril (cargo)	1964	1048	220	39	13
Fenella "	1951	1019	223	37	12
Conister "	1921	411	150	24	9

Postcard size photographs of the above passenger vessels may be purchased (4d each) from our Catering Department, Royal Buildings, Douglas, Isle of Man.

A booklet giving a history of this Company entitled "Ships of The Isle of Man Steam Packet Co. Ltd." by Mr. Fred Henry, can also be obtained from the Catering Department at a cost of 4/- (3/6d plus 6d postage).

Isle of Man Steam Packet 1963 fleet list.

The Mayor and Mayoress of Douglas greet passengers arriving on *Manxman* (1955/2,495grt) which was the first passenger vessel to arrive at the Island on 2 July 1966 following the six week national seamans strike.

1966 "FESTIVAL OF FUN"
REVISED EVENTS FOR SEPTEMBER

Event	Date
*International Old Time Dance Congress — Douglas	27 Aug —3 Sept.
*International T.T. Races	28, 31 Aug. & 2 Sept.
Dancing and General Entertainment — Villa Marina	to 17 Sept
Motor Cycle Scramble — West Kimmeragh nr. Ramsey	1
T.T. Gmykhana — Onchan	30 Sept. & 1 Sept.
Flower and Horticultural Show — Ramsey	1
Vintage Motor Cycle Rally	1
Motor Cycle Gymkhana — Ramsey	3
Golf Competition — 4 Ball Better Ball — Ramsey	3
Two Day Trial (motor cycle)	3 & 4
Isle of Man Treasure Hunt — £3,000 in cash prizes	3—10
Angling Competitions at Peel	3, 10 & 17
"Club-Land"—Palace, Douglas — Palace of Varieties and Old Time Music Hall	3—24
Golf Competition—Fort Island Cup — Castletown	4
Golf Competition—Morris Forrester Cup — Howstrake	4
Mannin Angling Festival (Southern) salt water, boat and shore competitions	4—10
Go-Kart and Motor Cycle Gymkhana — Onchan	5
M.G.P. Practices (motor cycle)	5—12
SWEARING IN OF SIR PETER HYLA GAWNE STALLARD K.C.M.G., C.V.O., M.B.E. AS LIEUTENANT GOVERNOR OF THE ISLE OF MAN — Castle Rushen	7
Isle of Man Treasure Hunt — £3,000 in cash prizes	10—17
Golf Competition—4 Ball better ball — Ramsey	11—12
Racing under Floodlight — Onchan	12
Angling Competitions by boat from Ferry Steps, Douglas	12 & 14
Manx Grand Prix Races Presentations — Villa Marina	13 & 15
Cavalcade of Speed — Onchan	14
Finals of Bathing Beauty Competitions	14
Special Night — Ramsey — Water Pageant, dancing, fireworks	14
Wrestling — Villa Marina	14 & 24
Manx Trophy Car Rally	16, 17 & 18
Isle of Man Treasure Hunt £3,000 in cash prizes	17—24
Golf Competition—18 hole Stableford — Ramsey	18
Billy Cotton's Band Show — Villa Marina	19—23
Hughie Green's Show — Douglas	19—24
L.A.C. Motor Car Hill Climb	24 & 25
Isle of Man Treasure Hunt — £1,000 in cash prizes	24—30
Vintage Motor Cycle Exhibition — Douglas	until late Sept.
Bridge Congress — Balqueen, Port St. Mary	24
"Night Out in Douglas" — Gaiety Theatre, Douglas	26, 27, 30
T.W.G. Pageant "Fashion Thro' the Ages" — Villa Marina	27
Choral Evening — Villa Marina	28
Isle of Man Open Badminton Tournament — Douglas	30 Sept—1 Oct.

— V.P. LTD. —

'Festival of Fun' programme for September 1966, including the swearing in of Sir Peter Hyla Gawne Stallard as Lieutenant Governor of the Isle of Man.

Mona's Isle (1951/2,491grt) berthed at the Battery Pier with Douglas Head in the background.

Manxman(1955/2,495grt) passes *Tynwald* (1947/2,493grt) and *King Orry* (1946/2,485grt) as she prepares to berth at the Edward Pier on a sailing from Belfast.

THE ISLE OF MAN STEAM PACKET COMPANY LIMITED
(Incorporated in the Isle of Man)

ENJOY THE LEISURE AND SEA BREEZES AND VISIT THE GLORIOUS

ISLE OF MAN

ON A DELIGHTFUL DAY EXCURSION BY ONE OF THE LARGE, FAST, MODERN STEAMERS OF THE ISLE OF MAN STEAM PACKET COMPANY LIMITED

ALLOWING ABOUT 4 HOURS ASHORE

(The Company may alter, withdraw, or curtail any service or suspend or cancel any sailing as the Company may think necessary)

S.S. "MANXMAN"

Built 1955 Gross Tonnage 2,495 tons Length 344 feet Speed 21 knots

LLANDUDNO TO DOUGLAS	DOUGLAS TO LLANDUDNO
JUNE	
Tuesday 23rd ... 10-15 a.m.	Tuesday 23rd ... 5-30 p.m.
Tuesday 30th ... 10-15 a.m.	Tuesday 30th ... 5 p.m.
JULY	
Tuesday 7th ... 10-15 a.m.	Tuesday 7th ... 5-30 p.m.
Tuesday 14th ... 11 a.m.	Tuesday 14th ... 5 p.m.
Wednesday 15th ... 11 a.m.	Wednesday 15th ... 5-30 p.m.
Tuesday 21st ... 10-15 a.m.	Tuesday 21st ... 5-30 p.m.
Wednesday 22nd ... 10-15 a.m.	Wednesday 22nd ... 5-30 p.m.
Tuesday 28th ... 10-15 a.m.	Tuesday 28th ... 6-30 p.m.
Wednesday 29th ... 10-15 a.m.	Wednesday 29th ... 4-30 p.m.
AUGUST	
Tuesday 4th ... 10-15 a.m.	Tuesday 4th ... 5-30 p.m.
Wednesday 5th ... 10-15 a.m.	Wednesday 5th ... 5-30 p.m.
Tuesday 11th ... 10-15 a.m.	Tuesday 11th ... 4 p.m.
Wednesday 12th ... 10-15 a.m.	Wednesday 12th ... 4-30 p.m.
Tuesday 18th ... 10-15 a.m.	Tuesday 18th ... 5-30 p.m.
Wednesday 19th ... 10-15 a.m.	Wednesday 19th ... 5-30 p.m.
Tuesday 25th ... 10-15 a.m.	Tuesday 25th ... 6 p.m.
Wednesday 26th ... 10-15 a.m.	Wednesday 26th ... 6-30 p.m.
SEPTEMBER	
Tuesday 1st ... 10-15 a.m.	Tuesday 1st ... 5 p.m.

SPECIAL FARE : 27/6 (One Class)

Children under 3 years of age FREE; 3 years and under 14, Half-fare. Infants must be accompanied by an adult. Day Passengers are not permitted to carry luggage.

All Fares are current at time of publication and are liable to alteration without notice

CONTRACT TICKETS: Available for 10 DAY-EXCURSIONS (£7 10s 0d) or SEASON (£9 0s. 0d.)

TICKETS, which may be purchased before the actual sailing day, can be obtained at:—

Steamer Booking Office, The Pier, Llandudno;
Stations of British Railways;
North Wales Travel Agency, 368 High Street, Bangor;
Beachcomber Travel Ltd., 9 Bangor Street, Caernarvon;
North Wales Travel Agency, Odeon Buildings, Rhyl;
Pickfords Ltd., 26 Abergele Road, Colwyn Bay;
Luxitours, 50 Conway Road, Colwyn Bay;
E. & C. Hindley, Beach House, Abergele Road, Old Colwyn.

THE DOUGLAS CORPORATION TRANSPORT DEPARTMENT offer you a **TOUR OF THE TOWN**, of approximately 1 hour's duration, taking in all places of interest—

T.T. Course : Quarter Bridge : Bray Hill: Governor's Bridge : Government Buildings, etc. Motor Buses are available on arrival of Steamer. Pamphlets giving itinerary of the "Request Tour" and tickets can be obtained from the Purser. Adults 2/3d. : Children 1/2d.

PASSENGERS AND THEIR ACCOMPANIED LUGGAGE will only be carried subject to the Company's Standard Conditions of Carriage of Passengers and Passengers' Accompanied Property as exhibited in the Company's Offices and on board its vessels. Acceptance of a ticket issued by the Company binds the passenger to these Conditions.

BREAKFASTS, LUNCHEONS, TEAS and **REFRESHMENTS** can be obtained on board.

Imperial Buildings, Douglas.   A. J. FICK, General Manager.
January, 1964.

"Courier" Works, Ramsey.

1964 leaflet advertising Liverpool to Douglas day excursions by SS *Manxman*.

Two views of *King Orry* (1946/2,485grt) as she turns off Douglas Head on a voyage to Dublin.

Mona's Isle (1951/2,491grt) crosses the bow of *Ben My Chree* (1966/2,762grt) off Douglas Head.

A Vulcan bomber flies over *Tynwald* (1947/2,493grt) as she begins a voyage to Liverpool.

Motor vehicles are unloaded from *Snaefell* (1948/2,489grt) prior to the Tourist Trophy Races in 1961.

Caledonian Steam Packet vessel *Caledonian Princess* (1961/3,629grt) berthed at Victoria Pier on a rare day excursion from Stranraer. She was sold in 1982 and moved to the River Tyne in 1983 when she was renamed *Tuxedo Princess*.

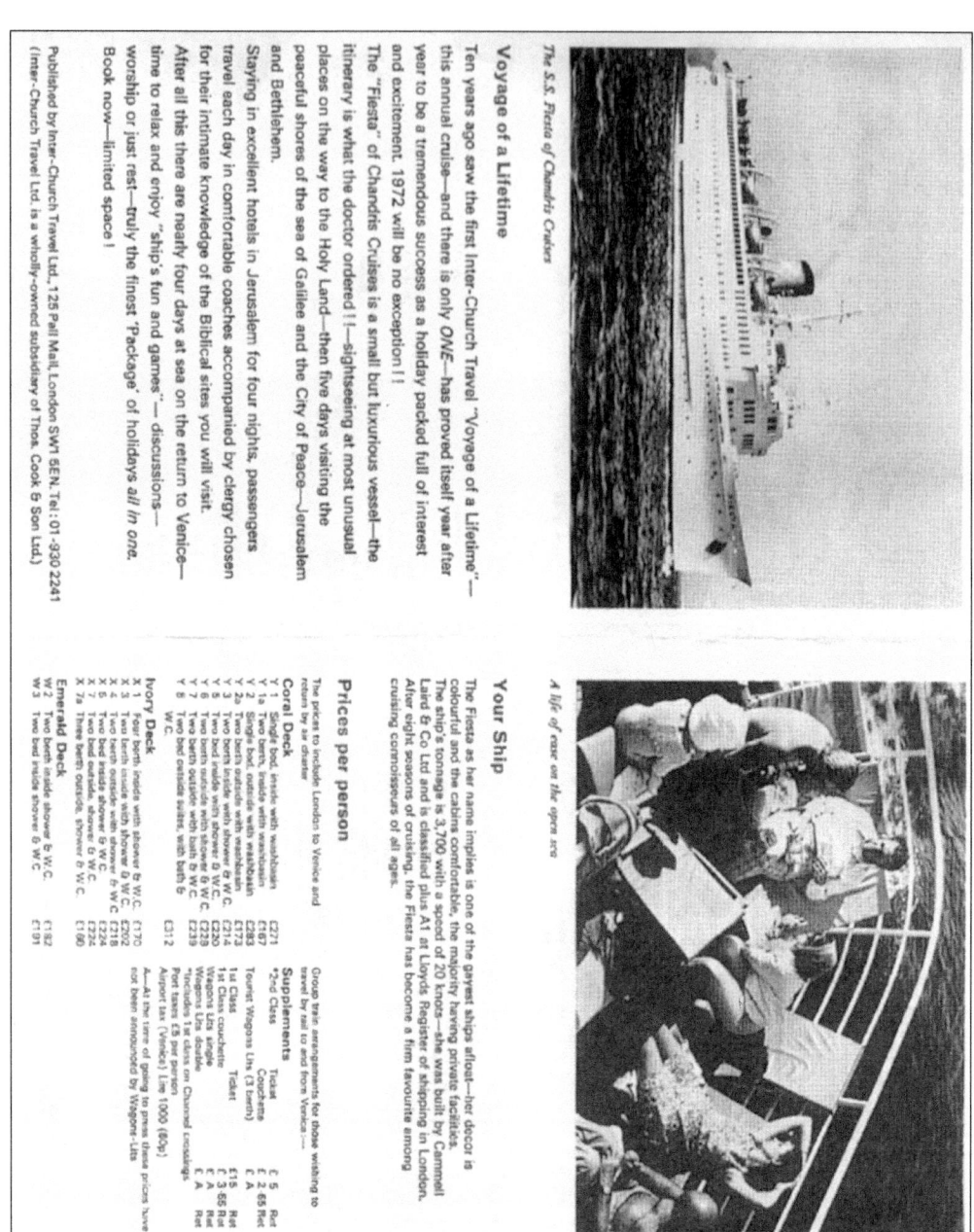

The S.S. Fiesta of Chandris Cruises

A life of ease on the open sea

Voyage of a Lifetime

Ten years ago saw the first Inter-Church Travel "Voyage of a Lifetime"—this annual cruise—and there is only ONE—has proved itself year after year to be a tremendous success as a holiday packed full of interest and excitement. 1972 will be no exception!!

The "Fiesta" of Chandris Cruises is a small but luxurious vessel—the itinerary is what the doctor ordered!!—sightseeing at most unusual places on the way to the Holy Land—then five days visiting the peaceful shores of the sea of Galilee and the City of Peace—Jerusalem and Bethlehem.

Staying in excellent hotels in Jerusalem for four nights, passengers travel each day in comfortable coaches accompanied by clergy chosen for their intimate knowledge of the Biblical sites you will visit.

After all this there are nearly four days at sea on the return to Venice—time to relax and enjoy "ship's fun and games"— discussions—worship or just rest—truly the finest 'Package' of holidays *all in one*.

Book now—limited space!

Published by Inter-Church Travel Ltd, 125 Pall Mall, London SW1 5EN. Tel: 01-930 2241 (Inter-Church Travel Ltd. is a wholly-owned subsidiary of Thos. Cook & Son Ltd.)

Your Ship

The Fiesta as her name implies is one of the gayest ships afloat—her decor is colourful and the cabins comfortable, the majority having private facilities. The ship's tonnage is 3,700 with a speed of 20 knots—she was built by Cammell Laird & Co Ltd and is classified plus A1 at Lloyds Register of shipping in London. After eight seasons of cruising, the Fiesta has become a firm favourite among cruising connoisseurs of all ages.

Prices per person

The prices to include London to Venice and return by air charter

Coral Deck
Y 1	Single bed, inside with washbasin	£271
Y 1a	Two berth, inside with washbasin	£167
Y 2	Single bed, outside with washbasin	£283
Y 2a	Two berth, outside with washbasin	£173
Y 3	Two berth, inside with shower & W.C.	£214
Y 5	Two bed inside with shower & W.C.	£220
Y 6	Two berth outside with shower & W.C.	£239
Y 7	Two berth outside with bath & W.C.	
Y 8	Two bed outside suites, with bath & W.C.	£312

Ivory Deck
X 1	Four berth inside with shower & W.C.	£170
X 3	Two berth inside with shower & W.C.	£202
X 4	Two berth outside with shower & W.C.	£218
X 5	Two berth inside shower & W.C.	£224
X 6	Two bed inside, shower & W.C.	£224
X 7a	Three berth, outside, shower & W.C.	£190

Emerald Deck
W 2	Two berth inside shower & W.C.	£192
W 3	Two bed inside shower & W.C.	£191

Supplements
*2nd Class	Train	£ 5 Ret
	Couchette	£ 2.65 Ret
Tourist Wagons Lits (3 berth)		£ A Ret
1st Class	Ticket	£15 Ret
1st Class couchette		£ 3.65 Ret
Wagons Lits single		£ A Ret
Wagons Lits double		£ A Ret
Port taxes (£5 per person)		
*Includes 1st class on Channel crossing		
Airport tax (Venice) Lire 1000 (80p)		
A—at the time of going to press these prices have not been announced by Wagons-Lits		

Thomas Cook & Sons Ltd Inter-Church Travel brochure for a cruise from Venice to Piraeus, Patmos, Kusadasi and Haifa on 7 April 1972 by Fiesta which was originally *Mona's Queen* (1946/2,485grt).

Tynwald was built in 1937. She was 2,376 gross tons and 96m by 14m with a service speed of twenty-one knots. *Tynwald* was torpedoed and sank at Bougie in 1942. (Keig Collection)

Another *Tynwald* was launched by Cammell Laird at Birkenhead on 24 March 1947. She was 2,493 gross tons and 105m by 14m. She survived until 1974 when she was sold to John Cashmore Ltd but was later resold and was broken up in Spain in 1975.

Mersey Beat Boat special 'non-stop beat music cruise' on *Lady of Mann* (1930/3,104grt) on 25 August 1968. The cruise was organised by Modern Musical Excursions as a tribute to Liverpool as the home of beat music in Great Britain. The cost of the ten-hour cruise was £2 with bands playing in three positions on the ship allowing passengers to dance, listen to the music or just relax and enjoy the atmosphere and sea air.

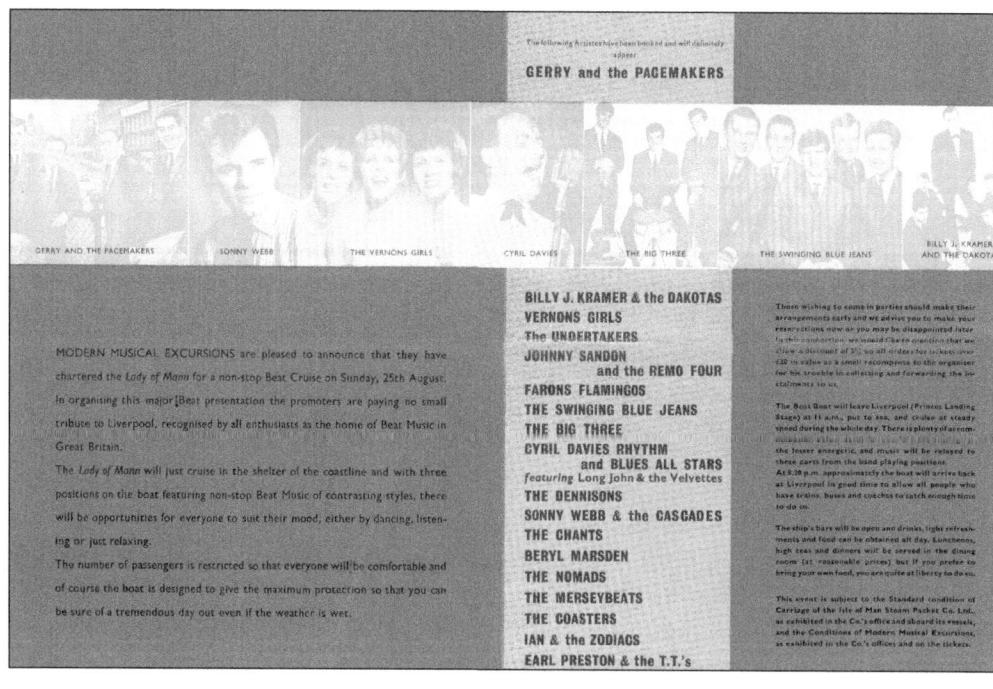

Manxman was built in 1955, 105m by 15m, with a service speed of 21 knots. She was sold in 1982 and was moored at the Port of Preston. In 1990 she was moved to Liverpool and to Hull in 1994. In 1997 she was towed to Sunderland where she was berthed at the Pallion Yard. In May 2002 the Manxman Steamship Company was founded with the aim of buying, restoring and bringing the *Manxman* into public use. The ship has now been recognised by the Greenwich Maritime Museum and has been placed on the list of historic vessels of great significance. The Heritage Lottery Fund granted the company £20,000 towards hull surveys and, on 29 September 2003, she was moved to the interior dock of the Pallion yard for preliminary restoration to begin. It is hoped to bring the ship back into pristine Steam Packet condition on the Mersey near her place of birth at Birkenhead.

Ben My Chree, built in 1927, 112m by 14m, with a service speed of twenty-one knots. She was broken up in 1965.

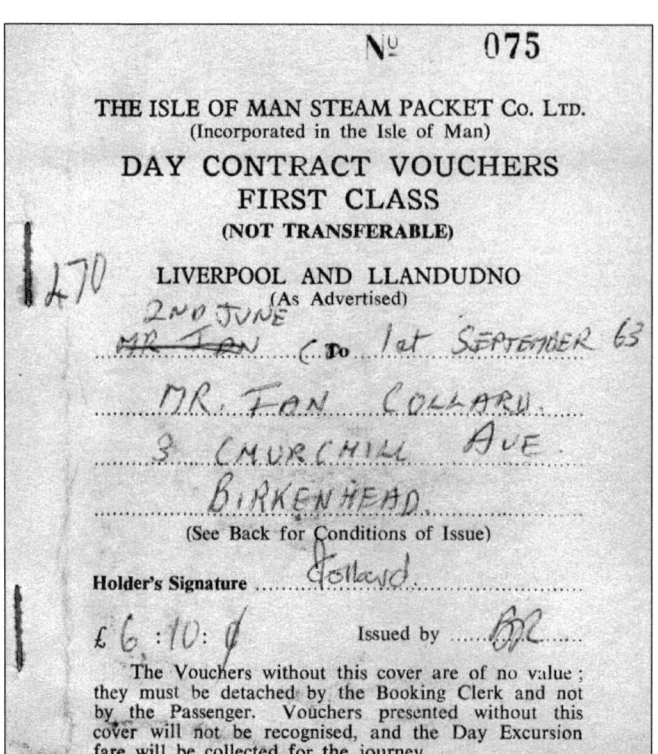

In the 1960s the Isle of Man Steam Packet issued Day Contract vouchers and contracts for use on any of the company's services.

Mona's Isle, built in 1951, 105m x 14m, with a service speed of twenty-one knots. She was broken up in 1980.

Snaefell, built in 1948, 105m x 14m, with a service speed of twenty-one knots. Broken up in 1978.

ISLE OF MAN SEASON – 1970

From: 24 Roby 1970
To: 17 September 1970

NAME	Liverpool	Belfast	Dublin	Llandudno	Liverpool Llandudno	Llandudno Cruise	Ardrossan	Heysham	Others	Totals	Charters to Other ports
LADY OF MANN (Capt. T. Corteen)	79	31	–	11	1	1	4	–	13	140	Barrow to D & rtn / Cruise to Calf / Cruise to Ramsey
BEN-MY-CHREE (Capt. E. McMeiken)	227	–	–	–	–	–	8	–	–	235	
MANXMAID (Capt. H. Bridson / W. Kissack)	221	–	1	–	–	–	12	–	–	233	(2 voyages to Greenock instead of Ard due to weather)
MANXMAN (Capt. H. Kinley)	66	9	17	25	27	9	11	7	15	186	Cruise to Calf / Troon Cruise / Ard to Bel & Rtn / Wark to D & rtn / Stranraer to Bel & rtn
MONA'S ISLE (Capt. B. Corlett)	61	–	21	24	19	6	15	6	7	159	D to Larne / Stranraer to D & rtn
SNAEFELL (Capt. J. Kinley)	66	5	21	25	12	4	9	9	8	159	Ard to Bel / Larne to D.
TYNWALD (Capt. J. Kennaugh)	43	16	7	16	16	2	19	11	4	134	Bel to Ard.
KING ORRY (Capt. B. Quirk)	51	21	10	19	16	5	13	6	8	149	
TOTALS	814	82	76	120	91	27	91	39	55	1395	

Statistical analysis of the number of voyages completed by Steam Packet passenger vessels in the 1970 summer season.

Ben My Chree (1998/12,504grt) arrives from Heysham as *Balmoral* (1949/735grt) and *Lady of Mann* (1976/3,083grt) prepare to sail on return excursions to Warrenpoint and Llandudno.

Laxey Towing Co.'s Douglas Harbour tug *Wendy Ann* at the south Edward Pier.

Associated British Ports 'Funboat' services from Fleetwood to the Isle of Man for summer 1988.

Lady of Mann served the Isle of Man Steam Packet for over forty years.

King Orry (1972/4,649grt) at the link-span on Victoria Pier, Douglas. She was sold to Moby Lines in 1998, becoming *Moby Love II*, then *Moby Love* in 2000.

Manx Maid was built by Cammell Laird at Birkenhead in 1962. She was 2,724 gross tons and 105m by 16m with a service speed of twenty-one knots. In 1985 she was sold and moved to Bristol but was broken up at Garston on the Mersey in 1986.

| TELEPHONE: 7080 BIRKENHEAD | TELEX 62463. | TELEGRAMS: CAMELLAIRD. BIRKENHEAD |

MERSEY RAILWAY : GREEN LANE STATION

CAMMELL LAIRD & CO. (SHIPBUILDERS & ENGINEERS) LIMITED.

Shipbuilding & Engineering Works

Birkenhead

IN YOUR REPLY PLEASE REFER TO

WJS/EC

26th November, 1965.

I. Collard, Esq.,
3, Churchill Avenue,
BIRKENHEAD.

Dear Sir,

    We now have pleasure in enclosing 2 permits for the launching of the "Ben-my-Chree" on Friday, 10th December, 1965, at 11.30 a.m. and would draw your attention to the conditions printed on the back of the permit.

Yours faithfully,

FOR AND ON BEHALF OF
CAMMELL LAIRD & COMPANY
(Shipbuilders & Engineers) LIMITED.

E. N. DODD Manager Commercial Services

Letter from Cammell Laird & Co. enclosing tickets for the launch of *Ben My Chree* on Friday, 10 December 1965.

Car deck and passenger accommodation on *Manx Maid* in 1964.

Passengers settle in on *Manx Maid* (1962/2,724grt) as she prepares to sail from Douglas to Liverpool.

PRIVATE AND NOT FOR CIRCULATION

THE ISLE OF MAN STEAM PACKET COMPANY LIMITED

Subject to Alteration without Notice

Sailing Arrangements — Friday, 7th June to Thursday, 13th June, 1985

N.M.P. Ltd.

B.S.T.	PRODUCTION T.T. & SENIOR T.T. Friday, 7th	Saturday, 8th	Sunday, 9th	Monday, 10th	Tuesday, 11th	Wednesday, 12th	Thursday, 13th
High Water at Douglas	0237 6.0 1508 5.5	0325 5.6 1557 5.0	0415 5.3 1651 4.6	0510 4.9 1750 4.3	0611 4.7 1856 4.2	0715 4.6 2002 4.3	0817 4.6 2058 4.6
MONA'S ISLE	H. to D.—0100—2nd D. to H.—1130 H. to D.—1700	D. to H.—0830 H. to D.—1415 D. to H.—1945	H. to D.—0100 D. to H.—1130—2nd H. to D.—1700	D. to H.—0830 H. to D.—1415 D. to H.—1945	H. to D.—0100 D. to H.—1130 H. to D.—1700	D. to H.—0830 H. to D.—1415 D. to H.—1945	H. to D.—0100 D. to H.—1130 H. to D.—1700
MANX VIKING	D. to H.—0830 H. to D.—1415 D. to H.—1945—2nd	H. to D.—0100 D. to H.—1130—2nd H. to D.—1700	D. to H.—0830 H. to D.—1415 D. to H.—1945	H. to D.—0100 D. to H.—1130—2nd H. to D.—1700	D. to H.—0830 H. to D.—1415 D. to H.—1945	H. to D.—0100 D. to H.—1130 H. to D.—1700	D. to H.—0830 H. to D.—1415 D. to H.—1945
LADY OF MANN	D. to H.—0730 D. to P.M. H. to P.M.	D. to H.—0500 H. to A.M. D. to 1500 H. to P.M. D. to H.—2355	H. to D.—A.M. D. to H.—0930 H. to P.M. D. to Belfast—1830 Belfast to D.—2355	D. to H.—1130—1st H. to Fleetwood—P.M.	Fleetwood to D.—1030 D. to Fleetwood—1730	Fleetwood to D.—1030	
MONA'S QUEEN	H. to A.M. D. to 1530 D. to P.M. D. to H.—2355	H. to D.—A.M. H. to D.—0930 D. to P.M. H. to 1830 H. to P.M.	D. to H.—0600 D. to Ardrossan—1530 Ardrossan to D.—2355			D. to Dublin—0820 Dublin to D.—1700	
BEN MY CHREE	H. to D.—0100—1st D. to H.—1945—1st	H. to D.—A.M. D. to P.M. STAND BY D. to H.—1945	H. to D.—A.M. D. to H.—1130—1st H. to D.—P.M.				
Wind and Weather							

Sailing arrangements from 7 June 1985 to 13 June 1985, detailing sailings by *Ben My Chree* which had been chartered back to the Steam Packet for the Tourist Trophy period.

Lady of Mann (1976/3,083grt) leaves Douglas on 28 June 1994 bound for Birkenhead Vittoria Dock and an uncertain future following the introduction of Seacat *Isle of Man* (1991/3,003grt) into service.

Isle of Man Seaways brochure for 1988 featuring *Tynwald*.

A view from the bridge of *Ben My Chree* (1966/2,762grt).

Acor Line whale logo painted on the side of *Lady of Mann* (1976/3,083grt) prior to her charter to the Azores.

Return ticket for *Guildcruise '72* from Preston to Douglas by *Mona's Isle* on 25 June 1972. The timings of the cruise and her subsequent sailings were as follows :

24.6.72	Douglas to Preston (p.m.)
25.6.72	09.15 sails Preston to Douglas
	18.45 sails Douglas to Preston
26.6.72	Preston to Fleetwood (a.m.)
27.6.72	10.30 Fleetwood to Douglas
28.6.72	17.00 Douglas to Heysham
29.6.72	Heysham to Ardrossan-light

Two

Ramsey, Ardrossan, Belfast, Dublin & Heysham

Snaefell mountain, in the Isle of Man, stands at 2,034ft; from the top one can see England, Scotland, Ireland and Wales. Passenger services were operated by the Steam Packet to Ardrossan, Belfast, Dublin and Heysham. The steamer took six hours to reach the Scottish port of Ardrossan, four and a half hours to Belfast and Dublin, and three hours to Heysham.

Many visitors to the island would arrive from one of these ports and others would include a day excursion to Belfast or Dublin in their holiday. Passengers arriving from Dublin would have to pass through HM Customs & Excise, a temporary post set up for sailings from Ireland, and declare any dutiable items they were bringing into the island.

The passenger vessels had four decks with promenade space on the shelter or promenade decks and a variety of comfortable seating was available. They were fully licensed and various refreshments were on sale throughout the voyage.

The timetable for the Belfast sailings included a call at the Queens Pier at Ramsey. However, in 1970, the Steam Packet announced that expensive repairs were required to the pier and that they would cease to operate these sailings. The final call at Ramsey was made by *Manxman* on 10 September of that year.

Mona's Isle (1951/2,491grt) approaches Ramsey Pier to unload passengers from Belfast.

Lady of Mann (1930/3,104grt) calls at Ramsey Pier on a voyage from Belfast to Douglas.

Mona's Isle (1951/2,491grt) berths at Ardrossan Harbour at the end of a sailing from Douglas.

Manxman (1955/2,495grt) passes Ailsa Craig on a six-hour voyage from Ardrossan to Douglas.

Tynwald (1947/2,493grt) anchors in the harbour awaiting a loading berth at Ardrossan.

Snaefell (1948/2,489grt) powers ahead at twenty-one knots as she sails up the River Clyde to Ardrossan.

Passengers disembark on arrival at Ardrossan.

The sun sets as *Ben My Chree* (1966/2,762grt) approaches Ardrossan Harbour.

A fishing boat passes *Tynwald* (1947/2,493grt) as she moves astern at the entrance to Dublin Harbour on a sailing from Douglas.

Below: *Tynwald* berthed at the North Wall in the River Liffey at Dublin.

Three

Llandudno

Llandudno is the largest seaside resort in Wales. It became popular in Victorian and Edwardian times when the railway enabled people to travel to the seaside for holidays or day excursions. The bay is situated between the Little Orme and the Great Orme and the pier was able to accommodate steamers from Liverpool and the Isle of Man.

In 1962, the Liverpool & North Wales Steamship Co. went into voluntary liquidation and the service was taken over by the Isle of Man Steamship Co. The Liverpool-based company operated three ships *St Tudno* (1926/2,326grt), *St Seriol* (1931/1,586 grt) and *St Trillo* (1936/314grt) and had been responsible for the North Wales service since 1891.

St Tudno had operated the daily Liverpool to Llandudno and Menai Bridge service, *St Trillo* ran coastal sailings from Llandudno and *St Seriol* was no stranger to the Isle of Man as she was used by the company on their Llandudno to Douglas service.

The Steam Packet's first sailing on the route was on Sunday 2 June 1963 and sailings were operated several times a week during the summer season. However, problems with the pier at Llandudno caused the cancellation of the service in 1967. Work on the pier was completed early the following year and the service resumed in the summer of 1968.

St Trillo operated cruises from Llandudno until 1969 when she was withdrawn. In 1970, the Steam Packet introduced two-hour cruises along the Welsh coast. The Llandudno service continued until 1980 when *Mona's Isle* was sold to shipbreakers.

The arrival of *King Orry* (1946/2,485grt) fails to disrupt a fishing competition at the pier head on Llandudno Pier.

St Trillo (1936/314grt) passes *Manxman* (1955/2,495grt) on her approach to Llandudno Pier at the end of a cruise along the North Wales coast.

Tynwald day excursion from Douglas to Llandudno on 6 July 1970.

Tynwald (1947/2,493grt) moves forward from Llandudno Pier to anchor in the bay and prepare for the return sailing to Liverpool at 5.15 p.m. that day.

Snaefell (1948/2,489grt) berths at Llandudno Pier on a day excursion sailing from Liverpool.

The Isle of Man Steam Packet Co. Limited

(INCORPORATED IN THE ISLE OF MAN.)

P.O. BOX No. 5

Imperial Buildings,
Douglas, Isle of Man.

TELEGRAMS: "STEAMERS, DOUGLAS."
TELEPHONE No. DOUGLAS 5224
TELEX 62414 STEAMERS, DOUGLAS

January, 1970.

Dear Sir or Madam,

    Now that we have entered into another year no doubt you will be looking forward to the coming summer season and I have pleasure in enclosing details of our sailings along with Contract Ticket Form. The sailings are on a similar pattern to those of 1969, except that this year we intend to operate a number of TWO HOUR AFTERNOON CRUISES from Llandudno Pier to Red Wharf Bay, Puffin Island and proceed towards Point Lynas. The sailings will be taken by the steamer on the Liverpool/Llandudno service and for those contractors who are interested we have arranged for a combined Liverpool/Llandudno Cruise Contract as per details on form. Passengers holding Voucher Tickets who may wish to make an occasional cruise can do so by purchasing a ticket at the Liverpool Landing Stage at a cost of 7/6d.

    I trust that we will have the privilege of your patronage in 1970 and if you have any friends who are interested or can give our sailings any publicity it will be greatly appreciated.

    May I take this opportunity of wishing you Best Wishes for 1970 and may we be blessed with good sailing weather.

    Yours faithfully,

A. Maddrell,
Traffic Superintendent.

Letter from the Steam Packet announcing the introduction of two-hour afternoon cruises from Llandudno to Red Wharf Bay, Puffin Island and towards Point Lynas.

Passengers enjoy the summer sunshine and sea air on the fore-deck of Snaefell (1948/2,489grt) as she moves astern from Llandudno Pier on a return sailing to Liverpool.

Tynwald (1947/2,493grt) arrives at Llandudno on a voyage from Douglas.

Harry Eaton's observations on the two-hour cruises from Llandudno and his tribute to the 1927-built *Ben My Chree* (4).

The Isle of Man Steam Packet Company Limited
(Incorporated in the Isle of Man)

OBSERVATIONS AND POINTS OF INTEREST ON THE TWO-HOUR CRUISE FROM LLANDUDNO

by Mr. H. EATON

BEN-MY-CHREE

No more will you speed o'er the Irish Sea
    To give great joy to such as we
Who trod your decks for many a year
    And gained a memory held so dear.

How loth are we from you to part
    Ben-My-Chree— girl of my heart
Such words indeed are marks of fame
    No other ship can be the same

Wherever fate shall point the way
    To other lands, or come what may
Throughout the years we'll think of thee
    Farewell, old Girl, dear "Ben-My-Chree."

                      H. Eaton

Manxman (1955/2,495grt) arrives at Llandudno Pier from Liverpool.

St Trillo (1936/314grt) waits for *King Orry* (1946/2,485grt) to leave the pier so she can load passengers for a sailing to Menai Bridge in Angelsey.

Occasionally two Isle of Man steamers would be anchored in Llandudno Bay. The top view, taken from St Trillo shows Snaefell (1948/2,489grt) which had arrived from Douglas and Mona's Isle (1951/2,491grt) on a day excursion from Liverpool. Below: King Orry (1946/2,485grt) arrives from Liverpool while Mona's Isle anchors following a sailing from Douglas.

A 1970 Day excursion leaflet.

Queen of the Isles (1965/515grt) operated a number of cruises from Llandudno in 1968. In 1972 she was renamed *Olovha*, *Gulf Explorer* in 1982, *Queen of the Isles* in 1987, *Island Princess* in 1992 and *Western Queen* in 1996. She was beached at Ranadi in 1997.

A view of the bow of *Tynwald* (1947/2,493grt) as she casts off and moves astern from the pier on a return sailing to Liverpool.

St Trillo (1936/314grt) was owned by the Liverpool & North Wales Steamship Co. and operated cruises from Llandudno to Menai Bridge and along the North Wales Coast. She was built as *St Silio*, renamed *St Trillo* in 1945 and broken up in 1972.

Lady of Mann (1976/3,083grt) at Llandudno Pier on a special day excursion, sailing to the Isle of Man on 22 May 1997.

Four

Mersey Docks

Mersey Docks had been the second home to the 'Isle of Man boats' for many years. Prior to the move to Heysham in 1985, Liverpool had been the major mainland port for the Steam Packet services to the Island.

Each year from May to September there were at least two sailings a day to Douglas and three-day excursions a week to Llandudno, North Wales. These were supplemented on Saturdays when most of the fleet were employed on the Douglas-Liverpool service.

In the winter months two vessels maintained the service to Douglas and the remainder of the fleet was laid up in Morpeth Dock at Birkenhead. Early in the new year the vessels would be moved into dry-dock for their hulls to be inspected and painted. This work was usually undertaken at Bidston Graving Dock in Birkenhead but other dry-docks were occasionally used such as Brocklebank and the various ship repair facilities operated by Cammell Laird & Co.

The first steamer would emerge from Birkenhead at Easter to provide additional sailings for the early visitors to the Island and by the end of May all the fleet would normally be out of dock in preparation for the Tourist Trophy races early in June.

Manxman (1955/2,495grt) passes a Birkenhead ferry as she docks at Liverpool.

Snaefell (1948/2,489grt) passes *Manxman* (1955/2,495grt) as she berths at Princes Landing Stage on a voyage from Llandudno.

Mona's Isle (1951/2,491grt), *Lady of Mann* (1930/3,104grt) and *Tynwald* (1947/2,493grt) berthed at Princes Landing Stage in 1961.

Passengers embark on the maiden voyage of *Ben My Chree* (1966/2,762grt) at Princes Landing Stage on 12 May 1966.

A busy scene on the River Mersey with *Remuera* (1948/13,619grt) ahead of *Manx Maid* preparing to sail on her maiden voyage for the New Zealand Shipping Co. in 1961.

Mona's Queen (1973/2,998grt) arrives at the landing stage ready to take the final sailing to the Isle of Man on 30 March 1985. The next sailing to Liverpool was a charter from Douglas on 3 May 1986. Some seasonal sailings resumed and in 1991 the company restarted the winter service to Liverpool after a gap of five years.

Mail and fresh bread is loaded onto *Ben My Chree* (1966/2,762grt) in the early morning sunshine at Princes Landing Stage in 1964.

PRIVATE AND NOT FOR CIRCULATION

VICTORIA PRESS LIMITED

THE ISLE OF MAN STEAM PACKET COMPANY LIMITED

Sailing Arrangements—Friday, 22nd August to Thursday, 28th August, 1980

Subject to alteration without notice.

B.S.T.	FRIDAY, 22nd AUGUST	M.G.P. Practices Traffic. Dance Festival. SATURDAY, 23rd	SUNDAY, 24th	Autumn Bank Holiday. MONDAY, 25th	TUESDAY, 26th	WEDNESDAY, 27th	THURSDAY, 28th
High Water at Douglas	08-39 4.5 21-13 4.9	09-44 4.9 22-09 5.4	10-37 5.5 22-58 6.0	11-25 6.0 23-43 6.5	12-09 6.4	00-27 6.9 12-53 6.6	01-11 7.1 13-38
LADY OF MANN Capt. Kennaugh	L. to D.—10-30 D. to L.—16-00	L. to D.—01-00 D. to L.—08-00 L. to D.—13-00 D. to Dublin—18-00	Dublin to D.—10-00	D. to L.—09-00 L. to D.—15-30	D. to L.—09-00 L. to D.—15-30	D. to Dublin—08-30 Dublin to D.—17-00	D. to L.—16-00
MONA'S QUEEN Capt. Quirk	D. to Belfast—08-30—1st Belfast to D.—15-00—2nd D. to L.—23-55	L. to D.—10-00 D. to L.—16-00	L. to D.—10-30 D. to L.—16-00	L. to D.—09-30 D. to F.—18-00	F. to D.—10-30 D. to L.—16-00	L. to D.—10-30 D. to F.—18-00	F. to D.—10-30 D. to F.—18-30 F. to D.—p.m.
BEN-MY-CHREE Capt. Ronan	D. to L.—09-00 L. to D.—15-30	D. to L.—06-00 L. to D.—11-00—2nd D. to F.—16-30	F. to D.—10-30 D. to F.—18-00	F. to D.—10-30 D. to L.—16-00 L. to D.—p.m.	D. to Belfast—08-30 Belfast to D.—15-00	D. to L.—09-00 L. to D.—15-30	D. to L.—09-00 L. to D.—15-30
MANX MAID Capts. Bridson/Faragher	D. to Ard—08-30 Ard. to D.—15-30	D. to Ard—08-30 L. to D.—15-30	D. to L.—09-00 L. to D.—16-00	D. to L.—a.m. L. to D.—10-30 D. to F.—18-00	L. to D.—10-30 D. to F.—18-00	F. to D.—10-30 D. to L.—16-00	L. to D.—10-30
MANXMAN Capt. Kinley	D. to Belfast—08-30—2nd Belfast to D.—15-00—1st D. to L.—p.m.	L. to D.—11-00—1st	D. to Workington—a.m.	Town Band Charter Workington to D.—10-00 D. to Workington—19-30	Workington to D.—a.m. D. to Llandudno—17-30	Llandudno to D.—10-15	
MONA'S ISLE Capt. Corrin	D. to Dublin—08-30 Dublin to D.—17-00	D. to L.—09-00		L. to Llandudno—a.m. Llandudno to D.—10-15 D. to Llandudno—17-30	Llandudno to D.—10-15	D. to Llandudno—18-00 Llandudno to L.—p.m.	DOCK
PEVERIL Capts. Adams/Hall	L. to D.—17-00				D. to L.—13-00	D. to L.—17-00	D. to L.—15-00
CONISTER Capts. Cowin/Adams	D. to L.—20-00			L. to D.—17-00	L. to D.—17-00	D. to L.—15-00	L. to D.—17-00
Wind and Weather							

Official sailing arrangements from 22 August to 28 August 1980.

Queen of the Isles (1965/515grt), *Ben My Chree* (1966/2,762grt) and the Canadian Pacific liner *Empress of Canada* (1961/27,284grt) at Princes Landing Stage in 1968.

Empress of England (1957/25,585grt) berths astern of *Snaefell* (1948/2,489grt) at the Landing Stage.

Manx Maid (1962/2,724grt) departs from Liverpool to Douglas.

Finished with engines *Mona's Isle* (1951/2,491grt) arrives at Birkenhead Docks at the end of the 1968 summer season.

Ben My Chree (1927/2,586grt) and *Lady of Mann* (1930/3,104grt) at the Landing Stage.

Ben My Chree (1966/2,762grt) and *Manx Maid* (1962/2,724grt) berthed together at Princess Landing Stage.

PASSENGER FARES

	Single	Return
Douglas and Liverpool	44/6d	75/6d
Douglas and Ardrossan	52/-d	83/-d

MID-WEEK TICKETS BETWEEN
LIVERPOOL AND DOUGLAS
65/6d.

These tickets will be available for travel outwards on Tuesday, Wednesday or Thursday, and return on either Tuesday, Wednesday or Thursday within a period of three months.

CHILDREN under 3 years of age FREE; 3 years and under 14 years HALF-FARE. Infants must be accompanied by an adult.

BELFAST and DOUGLAS
A limited number of cars are conveyed on the ordinary passenger steamers. Please ask for special handbill giving details.

RESERVATIONS

Vehicle and Passenger Bookings should be made as follows:—

Liverpool to Douglas
Douglas to Liverpool
Douglas to Belfast
to
The Isle of Man Steam Packet Co., Ltd.,
Car Reservation Department, P.O. Box 5,
Douglas, Isle of Man.
Telephone: Douglas 0624, 3824.
Telex. 62414.

Ardrossan to Douglas
Douglas to Ardrossan
to
McBride's Shipping Agencies Ltd.,
93 Hope Street, Glasgow C.2.
Telephone: Glasgow 041 248 5161.
Telex. 77181.

Belfast to Douglas
to
W. E. Williams and Co., Ltd.,
82/86 High Street, Belfast.
Telephone: 29281.
Telex. 74619.

Your arrival and departure point in Liverpool is the Princess Landing Stage, The Pier Head.

Don't delay-Book today

S.S. "BEN-MY-CHREE"

Isle of Man Car Ferry

The Isle of Man Steam Packet Company Ltd.
(Incorporated in the Isle of Man)

Services 1968

S.S. "MANX MAID"

Passenger/Car Ferry brochure detailing sailings from 17 June 1968 to 4 September 1968.

Liverpool's famous Pier Head from the bridge of *Manxman* (1955/2,495grt).

Ben My Chree (1966/2,762grt) swings in the River Mersey at the end of a voyage from Douglas.

Manxman (1955/2,495grt) prepares to leave Liverpool Landing Stage on her last passenger voyage to Douglas on 4 September 1982.

British India Steam Navigation Co. troopship *Dunera* (1937/12,620grt) and *Empress of Britain* (1956/25,516grt) anchored in the River Mersey as *Manx Maid* (1962/2,724grt) arrives from Douglas.

THE ISLE OF MAN STEAM PACKET COMPANY LIMITED.
(Incorporated in the Isle of Man.)

CONTRACT APPLICATION FORM 1969

The Company may alter, withdraw or curtail any service or suspend or cancel any sailing as the Company may think necessary.

CONTRACT TICKETS

Available on the Company's services between Liverpool and Douglas, Liverpool and Llandudno and Llandudno and Douglas :—

SEASON — May 23rd to September 13th inclusive	£19 - 0 - 0
SIX MONTHS	£22 - 0 - 0
TWELVE MONTHS	£35 - 0 - 0

SPECIAL WINTER CONTRACTS BETWEEN LIVERPOOL & DOUGLAS

Valid for 3 months between October 1st and April 30th	£10 - 0 - 0
Valid for 6 months between October 1st and April 30th	£16 - 0 - 0

CONTRACTS AVAILABLE ON ALL THE COMPANY'S SERVICES INCLUDING ANY OF ITS ADVERTISED EXCURSIONS

SEASON — May 23rd to September 13th inclusive	£26 - 0 - 0
SIX MONTHS	£29 - 0 - 0
TWELVE MONTHS	£42 - 0 - 0

CONTRACTS AVAILABLE ON THE COMPANY'S SERVICES BETWEEN :-

LIVERPOOL AND LLANDUDNO	SEASON	£12 - 10 - 0
LLANDUDNO AND DOUGLAS	,,	£12 - 10 - 0
ARDROSSAN AND DOUGLAS	,,	£16 - 16 - 0
BELFAST AND DOUGLAS AND RAMSEY	,,	£16 - 16 - 0
DUBLIN AND DOUGLAS	,,	£16 - 16 - 0
HEYSHAM AND DOUGLAS	,,	£8 - 10 - 0

SPECIAL DAY EXCURSION VOUCHERS

10 Contract Vouchers (extendible on request) available for Day Excursions between :

LIVERPOOL OR LLANDUDNO AND DOUGLAS

Valid from May 23rd to September 13th between Liverpool and Douglas (except Saturdays July 5th to August 2nd inclusive) and as per advertised programme between Llandudno and Douglas. Vouchers interchangeable on either service ... £9 - 10 - 0

LIVERPOOL AND LLANDUDNO

as per advertised programme ... £8 - 10 - 0

The above can be obtained from the Offices of the Company at Douglas and Ramsey, or at the Offices of the Company's Agent at Liverpool, Glasgow, Belfast, Dublin, Morecambe or Llandudno.

The above prices are net, but when two or more members of the same family residing in the same house take full priced Contracts/Vouchers from the same date a reduction of 10 per cent. will be made.

SEE OVERLEAF FOR CONDITIONS UNDER WHICH SUCH TICKETS/VOUCHERS ARE ISSUED.

Isle of Man Steam Packet contract application form, 1969.

Lady of Mann (1930/3,104grt) passes *Tynwald* (1947/2,493grt) in the Crosby Channel as she returns from a day excursion to Llandudno.

Manxman (1955/2,495grt) berthed at the Wallasey Stage in the Mersey which was the site for the new Twelve Quays development that now provides river berths for services to Belfast and Dublin.

Ben My Chree (1966/2,762grt) passes the Royal Yacht *Brittania* (1954/5,769grt) off Langton Dock in the River Mersey.

Manx Maid (1962/2,724grt) prepares to enter service in 1968 following her annual overhaul at Birkenhead. Crew test her lifeboats in Alfred Lock prior to her trials in the river.

Ben My Chree (1966/2,762grt) prepares to sail from Liverpool as her sister *Manx Maid* (1962/2,724grt) arrives light from the Isle of Man.

King Orry (1972/4,649grt) passes the Royal Seaforth Terminal and heads into a force 8 gale on a winter passage from Liverpool to Douglas

Snaefell (1948/2,489grt) moves astern into the Mersey as she begins a day sailing to Llandudno.

Lady of Mann (1976/3,083grt) leaves Liverpool for Dublin to inaugurate a new service venture for the Steam Packet. The 'Lady' was replaced on this service by a new fastcat, *Superseacat Two* and later in 1999 by her sister, *Superseacat Three*.

Mersey ferry *Leasowe* (1951/567grt) arrives from Seacombe as *Manx Maid* (1962/2724grt) sails to the Isle of Man in November 1968.

King Orry (1946/2,485grt) dressed overall prepares to sail on the Steam Packet's first day excursion sailing to Llandudno on 2 June 1963.

Manx Maid (1962/2,724grt) in process of demolition at Garston on the River Mersey in 1986.

Ben My Chree (1966/2,762grt) laid up in Vittoria Dock, Birkenhead from 1984 to 1989 when she was sold to shipbreakers at Santander, Spain.

Snaefell (1948/2,489grt) minus lifeboats prepares to sail to the ship-breakers at Blyth, Northumberland in August 1978.

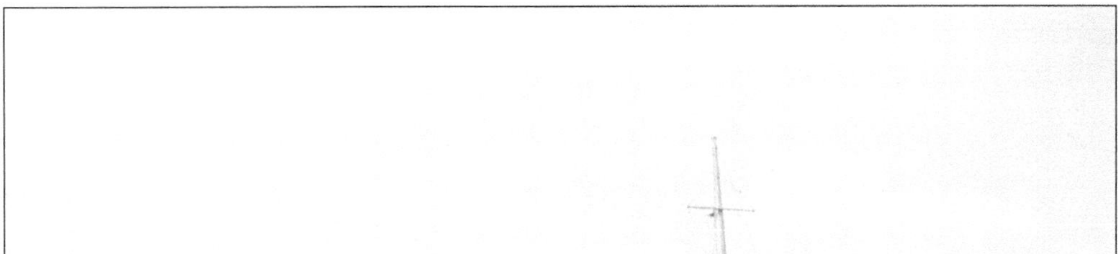

Manx Maid (1962/2,724grt) at the winter lay up berth in Morpeth Dock, Birkenhead.

A winter's scene in Morpeth Dock with the famous Mersey ferry *Royal Iris* (1951/1,234grt) and four Isle of Man steamers.

All tied up and finished with engines for the winter in Morpeth Dock at Birkenhead.

Tynwald (1947/2,493grt) in Alfred Dock, Birkenhead, at the end of the summer season 1964.

Manxman (1955/2,495grt) completes her annual overhaul at the 'cross-berth' at Vittoria Wharf, Birkenhead.

Snaefell (1948/2,489grt), *Mona's Isle* (1951/2,491grt), *King Orry* (1946/2,485grt), *Tynwald* (1947/2,493grt) and *Manxman* (1955/2,495grt) berthed in Morpeth Dock for the winter in 1966.

Mona's Isle (1951/2,491grt) enters Alfred Dock, Birkenhead.

Ben My Chree (1966/2,762grt) was sold in 1985 and chartered back to the Steam Packet. She is seen here berthed in Vittoria Dock, Birkenhead showing her port of registry as Liverpool.

Manx Maid (1962/2,724grt) manoeuvres through the Birkenhead dock system at the end of the 1968 summer season.

A view of Birkenhead docks in 1965 and the river waterfront including the Royal Liver Building at the Pier Head in Liverpool. The car-ferry *Manx Maid* can be seen at the north end of Princes Landing Stage and five classic Manx steamers are berthed in Morpeth Dock.

Morpeth Dock in the winter sunshine with Manx steamers and Wallasey and Birkenhead ferries at their winter lay-up berths.

King Orry (1946/2,485grt) and *Mona's Isle* (1951/2,491grt) dock at Birkenhead at the end of the summer season.

Ben My Chree (1966/2,762grt) and *Snaefell* (1948/2,489grt).

Lady of Mann (1930/3,104grt) with tugs of the Alexandra Towing Co. in Alfred Dock, Birkenhead.

King Orry (1946/2,485grt) steams up and tests her engines prior to entering service in 1966.

Three generations of Steam Packet vessels together in Birkenhead Docks in 1986. *Lady of Mann* (1976/3,083grt) manoeuvres past *Mona's Isle* (1966/4,657grt) and *Ben My Chree* (1966/2,762grt).

Tynwald was built in 1967 as the *Antrim Princess* for the Caledonian Steam Packet. She is 113m by 17m, with a service speed of nineteen-and-a-half knots. She became *Tynwald* in 1985 and was sold in 1990 and renamed *Lauro Express*. In 2003 she became *Giuseppe D'Abundo*.

Al Fahad ex *Mona's Isle* (1966/4,657grt) pictured at Birkenhead in February 1986 prior to leaving for further service for Saudi Arabian owners.

Free Enterprise 111, renamed *Tamira* in 1984 and *Mona's Isle* in 1985.

Lady of Mann was built by the Ailsa Shipbuilding Co. at Troon, Scotland, in 1976. She is 3,083 gross tons and 104m by 17m, with a service speed of twenty-one knots. She is still part of the Steam Packet fleet and was brought up to SOLAS standards by Cammel Laird at Birkenhead in the summer of 2001.

Mona's Queen was also built by the Ailsa Shipbuilding Co. at Troon in Scotland. She was completed in 1973 and is 2,998 gross tons. Her final voyage for the Steam Packet was on 3 September 1990 and she was laid up at Birkenhead until she was sold and renamed *Mary The Queen* in 1995.

Ben My Chree (1966/2,762grt) and *Manx Maid* (1962/2,724grt) laid up in Vittoria Dock, Birkenhead.

Lady of Mann (1976/3,083grt) and *Mona's Queen* (1973/2,998grt) at the same berth.

Channel Entente (1972/4649grt) is renamed *King Orry* following an extensive overhaul and repainting in 1990.

Tug *Salthouse* eases *Manx Maid* (1962/2,724grt) through the locks at Birkenhead.

In 1982 *Manxman* (1955/2,495grt) became the Russian ship *Moskva* in the film *Yentl*. She is seen here being repainted in the Steam Packet colours following completion of the charter.

King Orry (1972/4,649grt), Peveril (1971/1,975grt) and *Picasso* (1977/5,669grt) in Vittoria Dock.

A view from the upper bridge of the *Snaefell* (1948/2,489grt) when she was berthed in the East Float at Birkenhead prior to a refit in Bidston Graving Dock.

Claymore (1978/1,871grt) was built for Caledonian MacBrayne and was bought by Seacontainers for a new service from Scotland to Northern Ireland. She also completed a number of sailings for the Steam Packet during Tourist Trophy weeks. However, her main route was axed in 2000 and she was laid up in Vittoria Dock at Birkenhead.

Manx Viking (1976/3,589grt) was built as the *Monte Castillo* for Naveria Aznar, Spain, and was renamed in 1978. She was sold in 1986 becoming the *Skudenes*, and then the *Nindawayma* in 1989.

Mona's Queen (1973/2,998grt), *Lady of Mann* (1976/3,083grt) and *Ben My Chree* (1966/2,762grt) in Vittoria Dock, Birkenhead.

Mona's Queen (1973/2,998grt) and Stena Line *Stena Sea Lynx II* (1994/3,989grt) berthed together in Vittoria Dock. *Stena Sea Lynx II* became *Stena Lynx* in 1995, *Ronda Marina* in 1998 and *Incat 033* in 2000. In 2004, as *Thundercat 2*, she was laid up at Malta and is for sale.

Tynwald (1967/3,762grt), *Mona's Queen* (1973/2,998grt) and *Lady of Mann* (1976/3,083grt) in Bidston Dock, Birkenhead.

King Orry (1972/4,649grt) passes New Brighton at the end of a voyage from Douglas.

Lady of Mann (1976/3,083grt) berthed astern of the Royal Yacht *Britannia* (1954/5,769grt) at Princes Landing Stage on the occasion of a visit by Her Majesty the Queen to Merseyside.

A small fishing boat is dwarfed by *Tynwald* (1947/2,493grt) in Bidston Graving Dock, Birkenhead.

Ben My Chree (1927/2,586grt) in Brocklebank Graving Dock, Liverpool.

A new radar system is fitted to *Lady of Mann* (1930/3,104grt) in Brocklebank Graving Dock, Liverpool.

King Orry (1946/2,485grt) has her hull painted in Bidston Dry Dock.

Tynwald (1947/2,493grt) is supported by wooden beams in dry dock while she undertakes her annual overall in 1961.

Manxman (1955/2,495grt) is prepared for a busy summer season.

Extensive work was carried out on *Mona's Isle* (1951/2,491grt) in 1964 following her grounding on rocks at Peel in the Isle of Man. This photograph shows a section of her stern and rudder being replaced in dry dock at Birkenhead.

Ben My Chree (1998/12,504grt) undertakes her first annual overhaul in Bidston Dry Dock, Birkenhead.

Ben My Chree (1998/12,504grt) in the same drydock in 2004 when new passenger accommodation was fitted to increase her capacity.

Five

Cargo Vessels

In 1951 the Steam Packet introduced the first motor vessel to the fleet. The cargo vessel *Fenella* (3) was built by the Ailsa Shipbuilding Co. at Troon in Scotland. *Peveril* (3) followed in 1964 and *Ramsey* (2) in 1965.

Peveril (3) was converted to a container vessel in 1972 and in 1973 *Spaniel* was chartered from the Belfast Steamship Co. and bought from them later that year and renamed *Conister* (2). The NF *Jaguar* was chartered from P & O in 1981 and a link span was built at the Edward Pier. In 1982 she was chartered on a long term basis and her name changed to *Peveril* (4). She continued in service until the arrival on the *Ben My Chree* (6) in 1998.

The Ramsey Steamship Co. was established in 1913 as ship-owners and brokers, Their first ship *Ben Veg* (1) was built in 1914 and survived until 22 May 1941 when she was abandoned and sank eight miles north of the Point of Ayre.

Ben Rein (1), purchased in 1916, had a short career with the Company as she was lost through enemy action on 7 February 1918; she sank thirty-five miles from Liverpool. *Ben Rein* (2) of 1905 was purchased in 1919 and sold in 1921. She was lost on 19 February 1941 when she hit a mine off Manacles.

The Company has traded in the Irish Sea with a variety of vessels and their present fleet comprises of four cargo ships registered in the Isle of Man. Known as the 'Ben Boats' each vessel has been given the suffix 'Ben' which means 'woman' in Manx.

Although these are the main shipping companies operating to the Isle of Man other coastal vessels trade in Manx waters. British and foreign flagships bring a variety of cargoes to the Island including fuel oil, liquefied petroleum gas, bulk cement and various building materials.

Fenella was completed in 1951. She was 1,019 gross tons and 64 by 11 metres with a speed of twelve knots. In 1973 she became the *Vasso M* and she caught fire and sank in 1977.

Conister, a 1932 Isle of Man Steam Packet, was 44m by 7m, and had a service speed of ten knots. She was built as the *Abington* and became *Conister* in 1932. Broken up in 1965.

Peveril, a 1929 Isle of Man Steam Packet, 798grt, 65m x 11m, with a service speed of twelve knots. She was broken up at Glasson Dock in 1964.

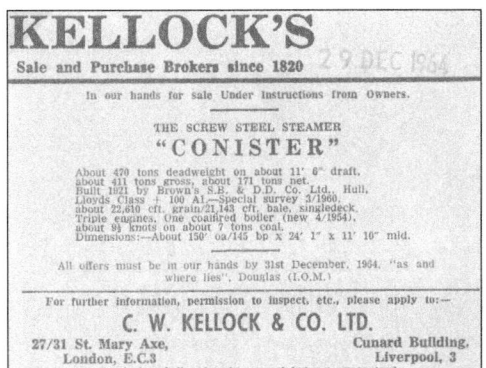 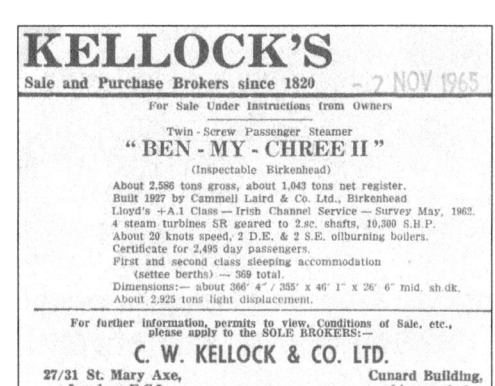

'Kellocks' sale-and-purchase brokers notices advertising the sale of *Conister* on 29 December 1964 and *Ben My Chree* (4) on 2 November 1965.

Ben Maye, 1921 Ramsey Steamship Co. (323grt), 40m by 7m, with a service speed of nine knots. She was built as *Tod Head* by J. Cran & Somerville at Leith, Scotland. In 1931 she was sold to R. Cameron of Glasgow and renamed *Kyle Rhea* in 1935. She was sold to Mrs Emma Cubbin of Douglas in 1940 and purchased by the Ramsey Steamship Co. in 1955 and renamed *Ben Maye*. On 15 December 1964 she arrived at Troon to be demolished by the West of Scotland Shipbreaking Co.

Ben Vooar was built in 1950 and is 427 gross tons. She is pictured in the inner harbour at Douglas in 1968. She was renamed *Arran Firth* in 1982 and was purchased by the St Ives Motor and Marine Co. of Panama.

Ramsey (1965/446grt) and Ramsey Steamship Co.'s *Ben Varrey* (1963/451grt) loading cargo in Ramsey Harbour. *Ben Varrey* was sold in August 1985 and was demolished at Millom.

Ben Veg, 1965 Ramsey Steamship Co., 346 gross tons, 44m by 8m, with a service speed of eight knots. She was sold to the Tyne Shiprepair Group and Brigham & Cowan in 1979, purchased by a Grenada shipping company in 1980 and went aground off the Bahamas on 4 August 1980. She was refloated and renamed *The Benn*; his name was altered to *Benn* in 1985. On 17 January 1991 she sank while being towed from Port of Spain to Castries.

Ramsey (1965/446grt), *Peveril* (1964/1,048grt) and *Fenella* (1951/1,019grt) in Coburg Dock, the Steam Packet's cargo handling berth in Liverpool until the closure of the South Docks system.

Fenella (1951/1,019grt) passes *Peveril* (1964/1,048grt) as she sets sail for Liverpool on a sunny summer evening in 1967.

The Lady Grania, 1952, Arthur Guinness, 1,152 gross tons, 65m by 11m, with a service speed of eleven knots. Sold to Halifax-Caribbean Shipping, Canada in 1975 and renamed *The Lady Scotia*, Star Ltd, Cayman Islands in 1979 and Naviera Industrializadora, Mexico in 1980. She was stranded off Cabo San Lucas, Baja, California during hurricane 'Carla' in 1981.

Fenella (1951/1,019grt) at low water in Douglas Harbour

Peveril, 1971, Isle of Man Steam Packet, 1,975grt, 106m by 16m, with a service speed of fourteen knots. She was built as *Holmia* in 1971, renamed *ASD Meteor and Penda* in 1973, *NF Jaguar* in 1980, *Peveril* in 1983 and *Caribbean Enterprise* in 2000.

Ben My Chree, 1998, Isle of Man Steam Packet, 12,504grt, 125m by 23m, with a service speed of nineteen knots.

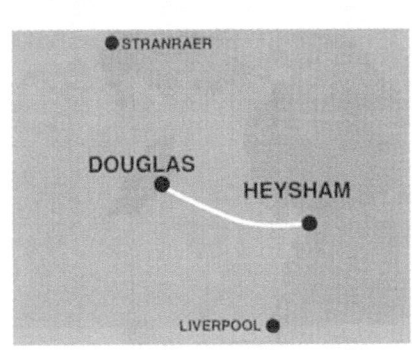

PORT OF HEYSHAM

The port of Heysham is our main point of entry to and exit from the UK. It's modern Harbour facility offers ample trailer space and two modern link span roll on roll off berthing units. The latest was commissioned in October 1991 at a cost of around £4 million. The port is well situated for the movement of goods North and South of the border. Heysham is within 8 miles (15 minutes driving time) off junction 34 of the M6 motorway. Manchester 67 miles; Liverpool 74 miles; Leeds 81 miles and Glasgow 172 miles.

SECURITY

Shippers using Heysham can rest assured their goods are in safe hands whilst waiting shipment. The port is fully enclosed, and security guards are employed at all times. We know the value of peace of mind to our customers.

```
THE STEAM PACKET
TRAFFIC DEPT. P.O. BOX 5
IMPERIAL BUILDINGS
DOUGLAS
ISLE OF MAN
TEL: (0624) 626503
FAX: (0624) 662757
TELEX: 627741
```

ISLE OF MAN STEAM PACKET

FREIGHT SERVICE HEYSHAM - DOUGLAS

M.V. PEVERIL

Publicity leaflets for the Heysham to Douglas freight service operated by *Peveril* (1971/1,975grt) issued by the Isle of Man Steam Packet Co.

Belard, 1979 Isle of Man Steam Packet, 1,599grt, 106m by 19m, with a service speed of fifteen knots. Built as *Mercandian Carrier 11*, she was then renamed as *Alianza* in 1983, *Mercandian Carrier 11* in 1983, *Carrier 11* in 1984, *Mercandian Carrier 11* in 1985 and *Belard* in 1985. She was sold to Aabenraa Rederi A/S, St Vicent in 1998 and retained the same name.

Theodora (1958/637grt) moves astern from the Battery Pier after unloading a cargo of oil from Heysham Oil Jetty. She was owned by Rederij Theodora BV, Netherlands and was sold to Spanish shipbreakers at Vigo where she arrived on 1 October 1989.

Ben Varrey was built in 1986 as the *Triumph* and was purchased by the Ramsey Steamship Co. in 2000. She is 997 gross tons and is 64m by 12m, with a service speed of ten knots.

Auldyn River, built in 1961 by Mezeron Ltd, Isle of Man (417grt, 54m x 8m, 8 knots). She was built as *Eberstein* and became *Claudia* in 1979 and *Auldyn River* in 1998. She was lengthened and deepened in 1975 and again in 1983.

Ben Vane is 541 gross tons and is 50m by 9m, with a speed of nine knots, She was built as the *Julia S* and became *Bulk Moon* in 1981 and then *Ben Vane* when she was bought by the Ramsey Steamship Co. in 1988.

Six

Fastcats

The future pattern of shipping services to the Isle of Man appears to be in the shape of fast catamaran vessels which operate at speeds of thirty-five knots or more. The Seacat *Isle of Man* was introduced in 1994 and now covers most of the Douglas-Liverpool sailings. Together with *Superseacat Three* she had reintroduced long day excursions to the Island which have proved to be popular and successful. *Superseacat Three* moved to the English Channel service and was replaced by the *Rapide* in 2001.

Seacontainers were the first large company to use fast ferries in Europe and South America, with Seacats that were the world's first car carrying catamarans. Hoverspeed Great Britain took the Hales trophy on its delivery voyage for the fastest crossing of the Atlantic. They are one of Europe's largest ferry company's operating services in the Irish Sea linking England, Scotland and Ireland. In 1999, they introduced a new fast craft service betweeen Heysham anad Belfast with a journey time of four hours.

Ben My Chree (6) is operating on a double daily sailing schedule on the Douglas-Heysham route with *Lady of Mann* supplementing the services when required at peak times such as the Tourist Trophy weeks in June each year. The *Ben My Chree* was built by Van der Giessen-de Noord in 1998. She is a ro-pax car and passenger ferry that can also operate as a freight only vessel.

In recent years, *Lady of Mann* has been chartered to sail from the Azores from June to September and in the winter of 2001/2 she will operate various sailings in the Irish Sea.

The Steam Packet now owns a modern fleet of vessels which were designed and built to meet the needs of the Manx people and their economy. It has changed and evolved over the years and is proud to provide a modern and highly efficient shipping service to its customers.

Seacat Danmark 1991, Seacontainers, 3,003grt, 74m by 27m, with a service speed of thirty-seven knots. Built as *Hoverspeed Belgium*, she became *Hoverspeed Boulogne* in 1992, *Seacatamaran Danmark* in 1993 and *Seacat Danmark* in 1995.

Seacat Isle of Man (1991/3,003grt) passes *Superseacat Three* (1999/3,500grt) at the Pier Head, Liverpool.

Superseacat Three (1999/3,500grt) passes Fort Perch Rock, New Brighton, at the end of a passage from Dublin in June 2000.

Seacat Scotland (1991/3,003grt) passes through the dock system at Liverpool following her 1999 annual overhaul in Canada Graving Dock.

Superseacat Two (1997/3,500grt) arrives in Langton Lock, Liverpool.

Seacat Isle of Man, 1991, Seacontainers, 3,003grt, 74m by 26m, with a service speed of thirty-seven knots. Built as *Hoverspeed France*, renamed *Sardegna Express* in 1992, then *Seacat Boulogne* in 1993, *Seacat Isle of Man* in 1994, *Seacat Norge* in 1996 and *Seacat Isle of Man* in 1997.